CANADA
REDISCOVERED

Robert McGhee

CANADA
REDISCOVERED

Illustrations
Gilles Archambault
Francis Back

CANADIAN MUSEUM OF CIVILIZATION

General editor
Claude Paulette

Editorial board
for *Canada Rediscovered*
Jean-François Blanchette
Francis Back
André Bastien
Louis Royer

Graphic conception
France Lafond

Iconographic research
Claude Paulette

Illustrations advisor
Francis Back

Photoengraving
Grafix studio (1973) Ltée

Production advisor
Henri Rivard

Printing
Imprimerie Boulanger

Binding
Coopérative Harpell

© Canadian Museum of Civilization, 1991
Legal deposit:
2nd quarter 1991

Canadian Cataloguing in Publication Data

McGhee, Robert, 1941-

Canada Rediscovered

Issued also in French under title: Le Canada au temps des aventuriers

ISBN 0-660-12919-1

Issued jointly with: Libre Expression

Includes index

1. America - Discovery and exploration. I. Canadian Museum of Civilization. II. Title.

FC300.M33 1991   970.01   C91-096314-2
E103.M33 1991

Cet ouvrage a été publié simultanément en français sous le titre *Le Canada au temps des aventuriers*.
ISBN 2-89111-484-1

CONTENTS

Introduction 7

Chapter 1 The First Peoples 9

Chapter 2 The Land of Promise of the Saints 23

Chapter 3 Vinland 37

Chapter 4 Helluland and Greenland 51

Chapter 5 The Search for Islands 71

Chapter 6 The Newe Found Islande 81

Chapter 7 The Labrador 93

Chapter 8 From Arcadia to Cain's Land 107

Chapter 9 Canada 123

Chapter 10 The Grand Bay 141

Chapter 11 Meta Incognita 155

Conclusion 167

Acknowledgements 171

Index 172

INTRODUCTION

Everyone knows that Columbus discovered America in 1492. But who discovered Canada? Schoolchildren in English Canada are taught that the country was discovered for England by John Cabot in 1497; schools in French Canada teach that Canada was discovered for France by Jacques Cartier in 1534. Children of both languages, however, assume that the discovery of Canada was a distinct afterthought to the earlier and more heroic discovery of America by Christopher Columbus.

Who Discovered Canada?

The truth is quite different. Canada was "discovered" by Europeans, and was a part of the European sphere of geographical knowledge, long before Europe knew anything of the more southerly portions of the New World. When Columbus landed on a Caribbean island in 1492, he was merely pioneering a new "southern route" to the western hemisphere. Columbus' explorations, and the subsequent conquest of New Spain, grew out of a set of geographical theories and incentives different from the ones that had much earlier brought Canada, and the "northern route" to the New World, into the consciousness of Europe.

Exposed as they are to the popular history generated in the United States, Canadians find it difficult to realize that Europeans attempted to settle eastern Canada almost 500 years before Columbus' explorations; that in the years after Columbus' voyage, Europeans were making regular ventures to Canada long before the territory which is now the United States had even been explored; that there was a European colony on Cape Breton Island a century before the Pilgrims landed at Plymouth Rock in Massachusetts; or that during the sixteenth century, Europe probably plundered greater wealth from the animal resources of Atlantic Canada than from the silver mines of Mexico or the gold mines of Peru.

The early history of Europeans in Canada is not only more heroic than usually credited, but also much more complex. We generally hear little of what happened between the time of Cabot's and Cartier's explorations, and the establishment of settlements in Québec and Atlantic Canada during the early 1600s. But the successful establishment of colonies was not the natural and inevitable outcome of the explorations which had taken place over 100 years before. The colonies of the seventeenth century were the result of experience gained in over a century of tentative settlement and turbulent exploitation. More importantly, successful European settlement was made possible by the decimation of Indian populations through a century of contact with Europeans and European diseases.

"Discovery" and the First Peoples

The fact of aboriginal occupation of the New World is tacitly denied by use of the word "discovery" in connection with early European exploration. The Western Hemisphere had long ago been "discovered" by ancestral Amerindians; it had simply remained unknown to Europeans until relatively recently. Yet the aboriginal peoples are generally treated by historians as simply another element of the New World environment, and as of little more relevance to history than were the beaver, buffalo or bears.

In fact, the First Peoples of the New World had an ancient history in the country, and had developed rich and cherished ways of life which they were quite capable of defending against occasional shiploads of Old World sailors or would-be settlers. Far from being irrelevant to Canadian history, they were the dominant factor in regulating early European penetration of the New World. They successfully prevented European settlement of Canada for five centuries, since the time that the mediaeval Norse first sought to establish an outpost of Europe in what is now eastern Canada. One of the most interesting and most consequential facets of early European experience in the New World, is the nature of the contacts and developing relationships between newcomers and original inhabitants. In such relationships, we find one of the keys to interpreting what happened during the first few centuries following the European "rediscovery" of Canada.

Early Knowledge of Canada

Another key that may help us better understand the sequence of events that eventually brought Canada into the dominion of Europe lies in recognizing that Europe knew of Canada long before the voyages of John Cabot or Jacques Cartier. Knowledge and experience of a "northern route" to the New World had been developed for more than 1,000 years before Champlain established Québec, or Lord Baltimore planted an English colony in Newfoundland, or Sir Walter Raleigh founded the first Virginia Colony.

This knowledge began to accumulate with the voyages of mediaeval Irish monks into the far reaches of the North Atlantic Ocean, voyages which may have begun as early as the sixth century A.D., and by the eighth century had resulted in the establishment of Irish monastic communities on islands as far west as Iceland. In their wake came Norse farmers, searching for land on the outer fringes of the known world, and finding it as far west as Greenland and Newfoundland. The colonies which the Norse established in Greenland lasted for five centuries, disappearing only about the time of Columbus, Cabot and Cartier. Throughout this lengthy period the Greenlanders supplied Europe with ivory, narwhal tusks, gyrfalcons, polar bear skins and occasional bits of information regarding new lands in the far west.

When fifteenth-century Europeans once again began pushing outwards across the Atlantic, there are indications that they knew something of what they would find, and the direction they should take to find it. There are also persistent hints that the official voyages which have found their way into the history books may have been based on more immediate knowledge: that John Cabot was following a

trail first opened decades earlier by Portuguese and English fishermen, and that Jacques Cartier's exploration of the Gulf of St. Lawrence only confirmed what French fishermen had already reported.

Canada Before Champlain

As awareness of Canada hovered on the edge of European geographical knowledge for five or more centuries before the establishment of successful European settlement, there were notable transformations in the way the new land was perceived. It may first have entered European consciousness as one of the *Blessed Isles* of mediaeval geography. News of its discovery reached Europe as stories of the Norse *Vinland*, a fruitful country inhabited by a hostile population. For most of a century it was best known as the barren and rocky *New Found Island* or *Baccalaos* (Codfish Land) of the early English and Portuguese fishermen. For a few years it became the fabulously wealthy *Saguenay* of Jacques Cartier and *Meta Incognita* of Martin Frobisher, northern equivalents of Mexico or Peru. Early European activities in Canada were conditioned as much by these changing perceptions, as they were by developing knowledge and changing technology.

The centuries before A.D. 1600 comprise an intriguing segment of Canadian history. Yet the period left remarkably few records from which we can reconstruct the frequency and nature of contacts between Old and New Worlds. Neither the archives of Europe nor the archaeological sites of the Americas have yet provided enough documents to construct a definitive account of European activities in Canada through most of these centuries. Any attempt to write a history of the period must be heavily influenced by the author's judgement and credulity in interpreting vague and haphazardly reported bits of evidence. The chapters that follow attempt to arrange these hints and clues to create a plausible picture of early Canadian history. It is a picture of two worlds meeting over several centuries, during which the perceptions, ambitions and destinies of Europeans interwove with those of the First Peoples of North America. This picture serves as the necessary backdrop for the eventual European conquest of Canada.

CHAPTER 1

THE FIRST PEOPLES

When Europeans first crossed the Atlantic Ocean they discovered a truly New World, a world whose plants, animals, people and civilizations were remarkably different from those of Europe. The First Peoples of Canada, whose ancestors had occupied and developed the country for 15,000 years, were the first native Americans to encounter the newcomers from the east.

A fine example of Northwest Coast Indian art, this club is carved from whale bone. It comes from the Nass River area of northern British Columbia. (Length: 39 cm)

Who are the First Peoples of Canada? Where did they come from, and how are they related to the other peoples of the world? According to their own beliefs, they were placed on this continent by a divine Creator, who gave the land and its resources into their care. Archaeology provides an alternative explanation, which pictures the aboriginal peoples of the Americas as simply the brothers and sisters of all other living peoples on earth. In order to comprehend this picture, we must look back to our Ice Age ancestors: the ancestors of all living humans, of both the Old World and the New.

This warrior, who appears in an edition of Champlain's Voyages, is probably a Huron. He wears armour made of sticks, as well as a shield which protected the archer when he turned his back to fit an arrow to his bow.

Our Ice Age Ancestors

About 35,000 years ago the world gradually entered the last major Ice Age. For the next 20,000 years and more, temperate climates were considerably colder than at present, and massive glaciers covered much of the northern continents. This period also saw the appearance of a new animal: *Homo sapiens* in a modern form, physically indistinguishable from the peoples who occupy today's world. This creature had developed the technology, skills and social abilities to be an efficient hunter of most other animals, and to live in most of the world's environments. The last Ice Age saw human populations expand northwards out of their tropical homelands, and take possession of most of the world. Some groups moved into far northwestern Eurasia, to become the ancestors of Europeans. Other groups spread eastward across the Bering Land Bridge, to become the ancestors of the aboriginal inhabitants of the New World.

Ancient Civilizations

Over the 15,000 years since the Ice Age, human populations around the world developed along hundreds of alternate paths to produce the cultural spectrum of the modern world. Local cultures changed at their own rates, in response to the environments in which they found themselves. Those groups which had an abundance of local food resources developed settled ways of life with permanent dwellings in growing communities. Agriculture was invented at various times in several different parts of the world, and each development led to rapid population growth and the establishment of villages and small towns. In areas that were particularly productive for agriculture, or that had access to other resources, these towns grew into the ancient cities of the low-latitude world: those of the Nile, Mesopotamia, the valleys of the Indus and Huang Ho, Southeast Asia, Mexico and Peru. From these cities sprang the intellectual and social achievements of the ancient civilizations: writing, mathematics, organized religions, professional armies, kingdoms and empires.

Although ancient civilizations arose on each of the major continents, they developed along very different lines. Perhaps the most dissimilar were those of Europe and the New World. These civilizations were built by populations whose ancestors had been completely isolated from one another since the Ice Age. When the descendants of these two peoples met for the first time, an event which occurred somewhere in northeastern Canada, humankind had finally completed its encirclement of the earth.

The New World in the Age of Discovery

What kind of New World did Europeans find when they first began to cross the Atlantic? Unfortunately, we know surprisingly little about it. Few of the earliest European explorers left more than brief and sketchy accounts of the land and its people. Most native accounts were soon lost, as native cultures were destroyed by disease and by European religious or administrative zeal. In many areas we are forced to rely on archaeological information, which produces at best a vague picture of past people and societies.

There is even considerable argument over the numbers of native Americans populating the New World at the time of European contact, with estimates varying by more than a factor of ten. Traditional estimates suggested a pre-contact population of between approximately 8 million and 15 million people in North and South America. More recently, it has been forcefully argued that these estimates did not take sufficient account of the massive numbers of New World natives who died of European diseases introduced within a few years of contact. Pre-disease populations of over 100 million

have been estimated for the New World, with up to 18 million people occupying North America to the north of the great civilizations of Mexico. If these estimates are correct, they suggest that New World population densities may have been on approximately the same scale as those of Eurasia during the Age of Discovery.

Iroquoian warrior in armour, based on an illustration from the works of Champlain. The armour is fashioned from sticks laced together with cords. During his visit to Hochelaga, Jacques Cartier was told of warriors who lived further upstream and who wore "armour made of wood and cords lashed and woven together."

This magnificent club is of a type used by the Indians of eastern Canada. It was probably collected by a missionary during the early seventeenth century, and was preserved in a French curio cabinet.

Tikal, in Guatemala, is the largest and most
impressive city of the Maya.
Its truncated pyramids, supporting altars and
high roof-combs dating from
the eighth century A.D., cover the vestiges
of several earlier constructions.

If New World populations were as dense as those of the Old, how did the two peoples compare in terms of social and technological complexity? Throughout history, the rate of social and cultural development of any human group seems to have been related to the individual environments in which these groups found themselves. In very general terms, New World societies developed somewhat more slowly than did the most rapidly developing societies of Eurasia. Although no one knows for certain why this was so, several guesses have been made. For example, the difference between the two hemispheres in the numbers of suitable animals available for domestication — especially draft animals such as horses, donkeys and camels — has been suggested as a factor that delayed the rate of New World technological development.

A more general, and probably more adequate, case can be made by relating differences in development rates to the simple fact that the Old World was much larger, more variable, and had a greater range of environments and cultures on which to draw. Old World cultures shared inventions and developments which emanated from the local civilizations of Europe and the Mediterranean, Egypt and central Africa, India and southeast Asia, central Asia and China. If each of these civilizations had grown in total isolation from the others (as did the civilizations of Mesoamerica), we might expect that the rate of development would have

This painting, dating from the early nineteenth century, romantically portrays Micmac Indians enjoying a life of ease in a bountiful land. The Micmacs of the Maritime Provinces and the Gaspé were well adapted to life on the ocean, using their sea-going canoes for hunting, fishing and travel along the coasts.

been slower, and would have approached the rates characteristic of New World civilizations.

Despite their slightly slower rate of development, the civilizations of Mexico, Central America and northern South America had existed for approximately 2,000 years by the time that Europe began to make contact with the New World. The immense city of Teotihuacan in the Valley of Mexico, which around A.D. 500 had been larger than Imperial Rome, was already falling into ruins. Jungle was rapidly reclaiming the cities of the Classic Mayan civilization, as the Toltecs of Highland Mexico extended their militaristic empire throughout Mesoamerica. A small and unimportant Mexican people named the Aztecs were rapidly absorbing Toltec culture, in preparation for overthrowing their predecessors and creating the largest Empire of the New World. In Peru, the Incas were similarly developing a huge empire based on military might and administrative sophistication. When the sixteenth-century Spanish conquistadors entered the capital cities of the Aztecs and the Incas, they were astounded at their size and grandeur, which put the cities of Spain to shame.

Canada's First Peoples

To the north of Mexico, relatively dense populations occupied most of what is now the central and eastern United States. These populations were supported by an agricultural technology based on the cultivation of maize, beans, squashes and other plants native to the New World. As far north as the Ohio Valley, farming communities supported towns characterized by large central plazas and massive pyramid-like mounds capped by ceremonial structures. The general level of social and religious organization of these peoples is reminiscent of the Gauls and Britons of 2,000 years ago as described by the Romans, who were then expanding their empire northwards at the expense of local tribal peoples. When European explorers found only remnant Indian populations inhabiting the ruins of large and impressive towns throughout the eastern United States, they assumed that an earlier race of "Moundbuilders" had constructed the towns and their monuments. In fact, the builders and their descendants had recently and rapidly disappeared because of warfare and disease resulting from early contact with Europeans.

The native peoples of Canada had developed ways of life which were adapted to regions of relatively cool climates and low agricultural potential, on the margins of the more rapidly developing cultures to the south. Estimates of the aboriginal population occupying what is now Canada range from approximately 200,000 to over two million, with the true figure probably lying somewhere between these extremes. The only regions of the country which did not support indigenous human occupation were the highest ranges of the western mountains, and the bleakest islands of the High Arctic archipelago. Elsewhere, local environments provided resources of fish, game and plant foods far more abundant than those of the present day. The natural food resources of most parts of Canada are mere remnants of those that existed before the past five centuries of increasingly efficient exploitation using technology of European origin, and by a large and growing population engaged in a world economic system.

In many regions it was possible to build productive economies and relatively sophisticated ways of life on these resources, using technologies that did not depend on agriculture or industrial exploitation. The prime examples of such development were among the peoples who inhabited coastal British Columbia and the adjacent interior river valleys. These areas probably supported a population of 100,000 or more people, living on salmon and other fish, sea and land mammals, and other wild foods. Plentiful food resources provided for dense local populations, occupying large villages of plank longhouses or huge multi-family pithouses. The social organizations and intellectual attainments developed by these groups were at a level of complexity characteristic of relatively advanced agricultural peoples elsewhere in the world. Their artistic accomplishment, including monumental art in carved and painted cedar, has been compared with that of ancient Greece.

To the east of the Rocky Mountains, most Canadian rivers drain to the Arctic Ocean and lack the runs of Pacific salmon which provided such a rich and dependable food resource to west coast peoples. In the Plains grasslands the bison was supreme, providing food, fuel, clothing and shelter to the 25,000 or more people who followed the immense herds. Since horses were only introduced to North America by the

The longhouses of the Iroquois were communal dwellings, each occupied by a dozen or more families. The houses described by Jacques Cartier were "fifty paces or more in length, and twelve or fifteen paces wide"

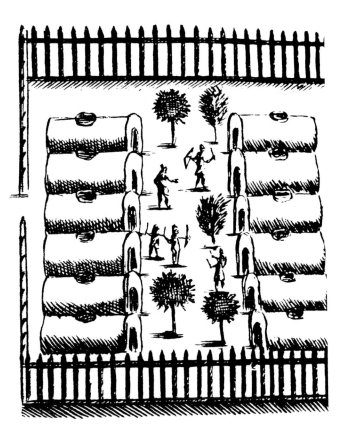

Baron Lahontan travelled to New France in the late seventeenth century. This illustration from his Voyages shows the characteristic shape of longhouses with rounded roofs, but little else about the village is realistic.

early Spanish settlers, aboriginal Plains Indians hunted the bison on foot, often by stampeding herds into log pounds or over steep cliffs or cutbanks. Archaeology shows that some of these hunting sites had been used for up to 10,000 years, evidence that the way of life which they supported was relatively stable and secure. New ideas were pushing northwards into the Plains at about the same time that Europeans began to arrive on the east coast of the continent. These ideas emanated from the agricultural villages which had been established in the Missouri River Valley, and attempts were made to develop an agricultural economy as far to the northwest as central Alberta.

North of the grasslands stretched the great spruce forests of Canada's northland, an environment which extended from Alaska to Labrador. This territory was home to perhaps 30,000 or more people; those of the western subarctic spoke languages of the Dene (or Athabaskan) family, while those of the east spoke Cree and allied languages of the Algonkian family. Both groups shared many common elements of a way of life adapted to the severe conditions of the northern forests. These were the peoples of the birch-bark canoe, the snowshoe and toboggan: hunters of moose or caribou, and trappers of the animals whose furs provided one of the earliest major European interests in Canada.

*The deserted city of Machu Picchu is a fine
example of Inca architecture.
In the century before the Spanish conquest,
the Incas of Peru had unified an empire
of several million people.*

The treeless lands and sea-ice plains to the
north of the forests were occupied by perhaps
20,000 Inuit, a people whose history was quite
different from that of the Indians who occupied
the remainder of the New World. The Inuit
were the eastern outliers of a much larger
population which lived in Alaska and along
both margins of Bering Strait, a people whose
ancestry and culture had closer ties to Siberia
than to North America. The Inuit of Arctic
Canada were recent immigrants to the area,
having arrived as the result of an eastward expansion from their Alaskan homeland. They
had come at about the same time that the Icelandic Norse established the first European
colonies in the eastern Arctic, and contact between Inuit and Europeans has been almost
continuous for the past 1,000 years. Yet the re-
moteness of their Arctic homeland, and its
unattractiveness to European settlement and
exploitation, has allowed them to persist as one
of the last American peoples to retain much of
their ancestral land, culture and way of life.

At the opposite extreme from the Arctic, the
most southerly area of Canada — southern Ontario and the upper St. Lawrence valley — supported a dense population of aboriginal
farmers. Perhaps 50,000 people occupied the
area between Lake Huron and Québec City.
These people spoke Iroquoian languages, and
their languages as well as their agricultural
economy and entire way of life were related to
those of populations to the south of the Great
Lakes. These were the most northerly of the
peoples who grew corn, beans and squashes,
and occupied large permanent or semi-perma-
nent communities across eastern North America between the Gulf of Mexico and the Great
Lakes. In the social and political organization of
the Ontario Iroquois, as well as in their religion
and view of the world, we can trace the ends of
cultural tendrils extending northward from the
civilizations of Mesoamerica.

Finally, the eastern coasts of Canada were
occupied by Algonkian-speaking peoples — the
ancestors of the Micmac and Malecite of the
Maritime Provinces, the Montaignais of the
northern Gulf of St. Lawrence, and the extinct
Beothuk of Newfoundland. These were hunting
and fishing peoples, with ways of life similar to

those of their relatives of the northern forest, but occupying an area with a considerably larger range and quantity of food resources. Like the Indians of the eastern seaboard to the south, and those of the Caribbean Islands, these peoples took the brunt of early contact with Europeans in the post-Columbus period. They were the first to be taken as slaves, to suffer decimation from diseases brought in the ships from the Old World, and to become inextricably involved in the economy and trade of early European settlement. Not surprisingly, they are among the peoples whose circumstances changed so greatly and so rapidly that little is now known about their aboriginal ways of life.

This, then, was the New World at the time the Europeans began to venture into the western Atlantic. It was a hemisphere with plants, animals and people which were totally new to Europeans, and a part of the earth whose human inhabitants had developed cultural traditions quite different from those of the Old World. In some ways it was an idyllic world,

with abundant resources and an absence of the diseases which caused so much suffering to Old World peoples.

Contact between the Old and New Worlds was first acheived in the northern portion of this hemisphere, that area which is now known as Canada. The First Peoples of Canada were the first occupants of the New World to meet the strangers from the lands beyond the eastern ocean.

The Western Ocean

The North Atlantic Ocean forms the western
horizon for all of Europe. Since the
continent was first inhabited, it has been a
source of mystery and wonder.
The past ten thousand years saw the gradual
development of human abilities to travel
and navigate on the sea. But only during the
last thousand years is it certain that
Europeans have penetrated the far reaches
of the Western Ocean.

When did ancestral Europeans first contemplate the Atlantic Ocean and wonder what lay beyond its horizon? For most of the past half million years, while the Ice Age glaciers periodically advanced and retreated across Europe, the continent was sporadically occupied by our early ancestors. These creatures had brains smaller than those of modern humans, but were competent hunters, tool makers and fire users nevertheless. Although they must have known the ocean, they almost certainly lacked the skills or ambitions necessary to venture farther than swimming distance from shore, and may have totally ignored the salt water, which couldn't even quench their thirst.

By the time of the last Ice Age, between about 35,000 and 15,000 years ago, Europe was inhabited by a fully modern form of human. These were *Homo sapiens*: people who created the paintings and carvings found on the walls of caves throughout the portion of Europe that lay to the south of the ice-sheets. In this artwork we find the first hints that humans were aware of the sea and its occupants: representations of salmon (which might have been known from rivers rather than from the ocean) as well as occasional depictions of seals, which are exclusively marine animals.

At the opposite end of Eurasia, people of this period had boats or rafts which allowed them to reach and settle Australia. Although sea levels at the time were much lower than at present, Australia was still separated from Eurasia by 80 kilometers of open water. While there is no evidence that Ice Age Europeans built or used boats, they almost certainly hunted along the ocean shore, and perhaps on the pack ice that extended from the western coasts of Europe at the height of the last glacial period. They must have created myths which explained the existence of the sea and its inhabitants, but we can only guess their thoughts on phenomena such as waves and tides, or on what lay beyond the ocean.

The First Sailors

The end of the Ice Age saw a rapid acceleration in the rate of technological and economic change across Europe, as in most other regions of the world. By 8000 B.C., as postglacial sea levels rose and the North Sea expanded, eventually separating England from continental Europe, hunting peoples living along its coasts began to develop an efficient exploitation of coastal and marine resources. After rising sea levels had finally separated England from Europe, the simultaneous appearance of new agricultural technologies and new artifact styles in England and Europe attested to continued contact with the continent by boat. By about 2000 B.C., watercraft were sufficiently advanced to be capable of carrying the huge "bluestones" of Stonehenge from their place of origin in Wales for a distance of at least 100 kilometers along the Bristol Channel, or several hundred kilometres around Land's End and up the English Channel to the mouth of the Avon River. Although these stones were probably carried on crude rafts, or slung between two large catamaran-style canoe hulls, their transport does indicate a relatively sophisticated knowledge and use of the sea.

Stonehenge, on England's Salisbury Plain, was constructed between approximately 4,000 and 3,500 years ago. The stones which form its inner ring were transported by sea from Wales.

Models and paintings from Egyptian tombs show that as early as 2000 B.C. the Egyptians were building large freight-carrying boats powered by oar and sail, but these were essentially Nile River boats which were too fragile for deep-sea work. By 1500 B.C., Scandinavian rock carvings show large boats which must have been used for coastal fishing or freighting. Sea-going boats are known from the frescoes and painted pottery of the Minoan and Mycenaean civilizations of the Aegean Sea, and it seems likely that similar boats were in use along most European and North African coasts before 1000 B.C.

Ancient Navigators

By the middle of the first millennium B.C., Mediterranean peoples were beginning to venture on long ocean voyages. The first to develop the necessary ships and skills were the Phoenicean traders living in a series of coastal cities in what is now Lebanon. About 600 B.C., the Egyptian pharaoh Necho II commissioned a small Phoenicean expedition to circumnavigate Africa, a voyage which was accomplished in

three years. The Greek historian Herodotus, from whom we have a record of this expedition, discounted the story because the sailors reported that for a portion of their journey, the sun crossed the sky to the north of them rather than to the south, as it does in Mediterranean lands. This observation, the first by Europeans who had passed to the south of the Equator, is now taken as convincing evidence that the Phoeniceans did actually reach southern Africa and probably circumnavigated the continent in the mid-first millennium B.C.

By the eighth century B.C., the Phoeniceans of the eastern Mediterranean had established a major city at Carthage, near the present city of Tunis on the North African coast, and it was the Carthaginians who carried exploration beyond the Pillars of Hercules (the modern Straits of Gibraltar) and into the eastern Atlantic. About 450 B.C., a Carthaginian admiral named Hanno the Magonid explored the west coast of Africa at least as far south as Cape Verde. He is said to have planted colonies in the area and certainly established trading relationships with the native populations of the region. There is also evidence that Carthaginian traders were moving northwards along the western coast of Europe by this time, and were trading for tin with the native peoples of western Britain.

"Ancient cartographers illustrated the perils and terrors of the oceans by populating them with fearsome monsters."

In their explorations and subsequent trading voyages along the West African coast, Carthaginian sailors may have begun the process of discovering islands in the eastern Atlantic. Ships driven by storms off the west coast of Africa seem to have discovered the Canaries, which lie only 100 kilometres offshore, and possibly Madeira a further 500 kilometres to the northwest. Local legends tell of a hoard of Carthaginian coins, as well as a Carthaginian statue, found on the small island of Corvo in the mid-Atlantic Azores group. These legends appeared soon after the Portuguese had settled the Azores in the midfifteenth century, but no coins, statue or other archaeological remains of early settlement have been identified, and it seems likely that these stories have their origin in local fantasy. The Phoeniceans were essentially coastal sailors, who probably felt uncomfortable out of sight of land and who had no motivation for exploration into the deep Atlantic.

Ultima Thule

Although the Phoeniceans developed the techniques and skills necessary for ocean sailing, other Mediterranean peoples made use of their growing knowledge. One such sailor, whose name has come down to us through the works of several ancient historians, was a geographer and mathematician named Pytheas, who lived in the Greek colony at what is now Marseilles. Around 330 B.C., Pytheas is reported to have sailed west through the Pillars of Hercules and then north, perhaps following the route of the Phoenicean metal-merchants who had established a trade in western Britain. Continuing northward, Pytheas came eventually to a land called Thule, which lay six days' sail north of Britain and one day's sail south of a frozen sea. Here he saw the midnight sun at midsummer, and was told that in winter the sun never rose. He described a phenomenon he called the "sea-lung," in which earth, water and air were mingled in a heaving mass that could not be navigated, and which suggests an unpleasant and distinctively North Atlantic mixture of fog and pack-ice combined with a heavy swell.

Pytheas' Thule soon became known as *Ultima Thule* — the most distant place on earth. His observations on the midnight sun, long winter night and sea ice, strongly suggest that Pytheas did indeed have knowledge of a far northern location. It has been argued that he may have reached Iceland, and thus become the first European to make an extensive crossing of North Atlantic waters. This seems unlikely, however, since Thule was described as being inhabited by people who grew grain and who also ate fruit, roots and honey, whereas Iceland seems to have been uninhabited until late in the first millennium A.D. Pytheas' Thule more probably lay on the western coast of Norway, a location which he could have reached using Phoenicean sailing technology and without leaving sight of land.

The Roman Empire adopted the Phoeniceans' nautical technology, as well as their overseas trade routes. In the east, they extended European commerce across the Arabian Sea to India. To the west, they knew of the Canary Islands off the west coast of Africa. However, the Romans do not appear to have been interested in Atlantic exploration or trade, and there is little indication that they continued the ventures of Pytheas or other early explorers. Some have suggested that the Romans may have reached Iceland, but the only evidence of contact is three Roman coins from the third century A.D., recovered from Icelandic archaeological excavations. These coins likely reached their resting places much later — perhaps through Viking looting of a European coin-hoard. In the absence of any written mention of Roman expeditions in the north or west, or of any other archaeological evidence of Roman occupation in Iceland or other Atlantic

lands, these three coins are not sufficient evidence to suggest early Roman voyages into the deep Atlantic.

As the power of Rome faded and Europe gradually entered the Middle Ages, the intellectual and economic energies of the continent began to be directed inwards. The geographical knowledge of the ancient world, including the concept of a spherical earth and the notion that one could sail westward from Europe to the Indies, was lost until the rediscoveries of the Renaissance.

Rather surprisingly, the first discoveries of lands to the west of Europe were not made by peoples who had inherited the knowledge and

Boats are common motifs in the ancient rock art of Scandinavia. This 3,500-year-old petroglyph from Göteborg in Sweden shows boats or small ships with high curved stem and stern.

technology of the Classical Mediterranean world. Instead, they were made by Northern Europeans — Celtic and Germanic peoples relying on native boat-building technologies and knowledge of the northern Atlantic. Their conception of world geography had little to do with the learning of classical times, and their motives for westward voyages were vastly different from those of the cautious Mediterranean traders. With them, Atlantic exploration enters a different world, a world of northern mists and ice.

CHAPTER 2

THE LAND OF PROMISE OF THE SAINTS

The Irish were the first Europeans to develop the abilities and the ambition to travel far into the northern Atlantic. By 800 A.D., Irish monks had settled islands as distant as Iceland. The legendary sixth-century voyage of St. Brendan has even suggested an early Irish discovery of the New World.

This silver chalice decorated with gold filigree and enamel dates from the early eighth century. It was found at Ardagh, Ireland, with other objects in a cache which had probably been hidden in order to protect it from Viking marauders. (Height: 18 cm)

The Christianization of Europe was a process which took over 1,000 years to complete. More than a religious movement, it was a phenomenon which consolidated the culture of the western Roman Empire, and gradually spread that culture throughout Europe. Over the first millennium of our era, it gradually transformed a great diversity of tribal peoples into a population which shared certain beliefs and outlooks on the world, and which shared access to the knowledge accumulated by earlier civilizations. Christianity was the basic force which produced the first truly European civilization, the "Europe of Latin and the horse" which we now refer to as "mediaeval." Surprisingly, it also served to stimulate early exploration across the Atlantic Ocean.

Holy Navigators

As early Christianity spread westward from the Middle East, different peoples took up the new religion in diverse fashions, each emphasizing a different manner in which to practice its teachings. In Ireland, as in North Africa, the monastic ideal became that of the hermit living in total isolation from all other human society. The Christian hermits of North Africa took themselves into the sand deserts, or isolated themselves atop stone pillars. The Irish equivalent of the desert hermit committed himself to the sea, with or without knowledge of a direction or a destination, in order to find an isolated rock or island where he could be alone with God and the devil. Three such monks arrived at the court of King Alfred the Great in 891 A.D. They had landed on the west coast of England, having left Ireland a week earlier in a small boat without oars and with food for only seven days, determined to serve God wherever He took them. Voyages such as theirs had been undertaken by Irish monks for several centuries previously, and some of these voyages seem to have taken Irishmen far across the Atlantic.

Ireland was Christianized early in the fifth century A.D., when St. Patrick founded a church and mission settlement in Ulster. The island became a stronghold of the new religion and a leading centre of Christian learning and culture. Throughout these centuries, monks set off into the surrounding ocean, eventually discovering and inhabiting many northern Atlantic islands. Using these islands as stepping-stones, they were the first Europeans who had the capability and the inclination to travel into the far reaches of the Western Ocean, and perhaps to make a landing on the eastern coast of Canada.

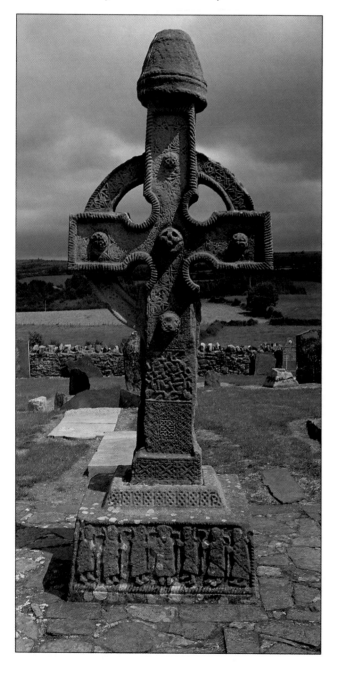

Monumental stone crosses, such as this example from County Tipperary dating from the eighth century A.D., are scattered across Ireland. Their decoration reflects a blend of local artistic traditions with styles derived from continental Europe.

An Irish monastery around the year A.D. 800. The monks did not wear distinctive clothing, and the buildings did not differ from secular structures. Since most early Irish monastic buildings were of wood, nothing remains except a few small churches dating from the eighth century or later.

The Curragh

The early Irish monks travelled in boats called curraghs, wood-framed with a covering of sewn ox-hides. Julius Caesar first described similar boats in the hands of the natives of Britain, and small curraghs are still used by fishermen of western Ireland today. Powered by oars and by a square sail, light enough to ride the largest ocean swell like a resting seabird, a well-built curragh was able to make extensive offshore voyages.

The seaworthiness of the curragh was recently demonstrated by the adventurer Tim Severin, who sailed a reproduction of such a boat from Ireland to Newfoundland in the summers of 1976 and 1977. His ship *Brendan* was 36' (11 metres) in length with an 8' (2.4 metre) beam — about the size of a small modern sailing yacht. She was built in the traditional pattern, using traditional materials: a light framework of ash splints tied together with 1,600 leather thongs, covered with 49 ox-hides tanned in oak bark and dressed with wool-grease. Although she weathered several storms, and was once punctured by ice, the *Brendan* made up to 115 miles (185 kilometres) per day and never put her crew of five at exceptional risk. On the journey they encountered the fog, icebergs, whales and other phenomena which are prominent features of the ancient voyage of *Brendan*'s namesake: Saint Brendan the Navigator.

The Voyage of Saint Brendan

Sea-journeys by curragh produced one of the most popular forms of early Irish folk-tale, the "imram," a fantastic sea-story which usually emphasized adventure at the expense of factual history. This pre-Christian literary form was soon adapted to the new world of the *peregrini*, the sea-wandering monks, and the most famous of such stories comes down to us as the *Navigatio Sancti Brendani*, the Voyage of Saint Brendan. Some scholars and Irish nationalists have argued that this story recounts the Irish discovery of the New World during the sixth century A.D. Such a conclusion is very dubious, but certain elements of the St. Brendan story do suggest that the Irish had knowledge of the central or western Atlantic at a very early date. It is worth looking more closely at the *Navigatio* — not least because it is a very entertaining tale.

The traditional date for St. Brendan's birth is 489 A.D. He led a long life dedicated to the Church, and founded several monasteries. He was also a great traveller, undertaking boat voyages on Church business to Scotland, Wales, Brittany, and perhaps to the Orkneys and Shetlands. In old age he was told of the "Land of Promise of the Saints," a blessed country located far out to sea and protected by thick banks of fog, which had been visited by an elderly acquaintance. In this fabulous country there was perpetual daylight; all plants were constantly in flower; all trees bore delicious fruit, all stones were precious; and one needed neither food nor drink, but constantly felt as though one were full of new wine. St. Brendan decided to undertake a final voyage in order to visit this wonderful country, and had a curragh built and provisioned for a journey of 40 days. Accompanied by 17 monks, he then set sail on a voyage which was to last for seven years, traditionally between A.D. 565 and 572.

During this extended voyage, St. Brendan and his crew encountered many marvels. On one island they discovered sheep larger than cattle, and on another nearby, flocks of birds which sang the holy offices in Latin. An island on which they landed and built a cooking fire turned out to be an indignant whale named Jasconius; the whale occasionally reappeared during their travels, and very considerately allowed his back to be used for several fire-less picnics. Provisions for their long journey were provided by various monastic or angelic persons discovered on several of the islands which they visited. They even located Judas Iscariot, living alone on a small rock and suffering everlasting torment. Finally, they reached a vast country and explored it for 40 days, eventually coming to a river they could not cross. A young man appeared, confirmed that they had indeed reached the Land of Promise of the Saints, and advised them to return home. Taking his advice, they returned to the sea laden with fruit and precious stones, and sailed for home.

It is difficult to identify the perpetual daylight, fruit trees and jewelled paths of the Land of Promise with any region of the known world. Among the miraculous and fantastic adventures of the holy monks, however, there are descriptions of more earthly phenomena. Stripped of their marvellous attributes, the reports of whales, fogs, rocky islands, wild sheep and massive flocks of seabirds paint a distinctively

North Atlantic picture, perhaps based on knowledge gained from voyages made to the islands north of Scotland: the Hebrides, Orkneys, Shetlands and perhaps the Faeroes. Other descriptions suggest that the ancient Irish may have had even more extensive knowledge of the North Atlantic. At one point in St. Brendan's travels:

A high mountain came up towards the north. At a distance it seemed wreathed in light cloud but the cloud turned out to be smoke belching from its peak. The wind carried them swiftly towards it. The cliffs at the water's edge were so high that the summit was obscured; they were as black as coal and wonderfully sheer, like a wall ... A fair wind carried them away southwards, and when they looked back from afar they saw the mountain, clear of clouds, vomiting forth flames sky-high and then sucking them back upon itself, so that the whole mass of rock, right down to sea level, glowed like a pyre.

*In the summers of 1975 and 1976,
the adventurer Timothy Severin crossed the
Atlantic, from Ireland to Newfoundland,
on the* Brendan, *a reconstruction of the type of
curragh used by early Irish monks.*

This sounds remarkably like a description of a volcanic island. Although accounts of Mediterranean volcanoes would have been known to educated Irish churchmen, the presumed North Atlantic position of this volcano strongly suggests that the description refers to Iceland.

A far northern location is also suggested by a report of the wind suddenly dropping, and the sea becoming calm and coagulated, suggesting a description of pack-ice. An experience with ice in another form is hinted by the following description:

One day after they had celebrated Mass, there appeared to them a column in the sea which did not seem to be far away, and yet it took them three days to get near it. When St. Brendan had come near, he looked for the top, but could see very little because it was so high. It was higher than the sky. Moreover, it was surrounded by an open-meshed net, with openings so large that the boat was able to pass through. They did not know what the net was made of. It was silver in colour but it seemed to be harder than marble. The column itself was of clearest crystal.

This would appear to be a clear depiction of an iceberg, surrounded by pack-ice or "bergy bits" broken from the main berg. Almost all large icebergs of the North Atlantic calve from the glaciers of Greenland, and drift southward with the Labrador current, eventually to melt in the warm waters of the Gulf Stream. They are most plentiful in Baffin Bay and off the coasts of Labrador and Newfoundland, and rarely drift to the east of 36° W longitude, in the mid-Atlantic approximately 2,000 kilometres west of Ireland.

In sum, the *Navigatio Sancti Brendani* contains hints that, by at least the ninth century A.D., when the *Navigatio* was written, the Irish had knowledge of Iceland and may have occasionally voyaged into the mid-Atlantic regions to the west. Any further conclusions regarding a possible Irish discovery of the New World must be pure speculation, based on the improbable and marvellous adventures reported in the *Navigatio*. There is, however, other and more trustworthy evidence to support the claims that early Irish monks did explore the northern Atlantic, and did settle islands as far west as Iceland.

Dicuil the Geographer

One such piece of evidence comes from a book entitled *Liber de Mensura Orbis Terrae* (The Book of the Measure of the World), a geographical description of all known lands.

This book was written in 825 A.D. by an Irish monk named Dicuil, who was employed at the court of Charlemagne. On the basis of personal knowledge, and of talking to other monks, Dicuil states:

All round our island of Hibernia (Ireland) there are islands, some small, some tiny. Off the coast of the island of Britain are many islands, some big, some small, some middling; some lie in the sea to the south of Britain, others to the west; but they are most numerous in the north-western sphere and the north. On some of these islands I have lived, on others set foot, of some had a sight, of others read.

The numerous islands "in the northwestern sphere and the north" must refer to the Hebrides, where the Irishman St. Columba had established a monastery at Iona as early as 563 A.D. They probably also include the Orkney and the Shetland Islands, the latter separated from the Orkneys by 80 kilometres of open sea. Archaeological remains of early Irish monastic settlement have been found on all these islands.

Dicuil may have been referring to islands lying even farther north and west when he states:

There are many islands in the ocean to the north of Britain which can be reached from the northernmost British Isles in two days' and nights' direct sailing with full sails and an

29

The North Atlantic

The North Atlantic Ocean can be seen as a huge circular organism, 6,000 kilometres across and up to seven kilometers deep. It takes its energy from several forces: the heat of the tropical sun combined with the freezing chill of the Arctic night; the winds and storm systems which brush across its surface; the rotation of the earth; and the tidal forces which twice a day pulse into the ocean from the south, gradually dissipating until they disappear 18 hours later among the ice floes of the Arctic. The heart of the organism is the Sargasso Sea, a weed-filled, sun-scalded oval lying between the Caribbean and the African coast. Around this heart circulates a massive clockwise swirl of water, out of which flows the warm artery of the North Atlantic, the Gulf Stream. This broad and rapidly flowing current carries subtropical water up the east coast of North America, across the Grand Banks, and northeast-ward to bring warm seas and a temperate climate to northwestern Europe.

Contending with the warm Gulf Stream waters, the pack ice formed in Arctic seas moves southward each spring, riding a series of cold currents which flow between Labrador, Greenland and Iceland. The ice which moves south of Spitsbergen in the Barents Sea, and which occasionally reaches Iceland, is soon melted in northern offshoots of the Gulf Stream. A massive stream of pack ice and icebergs flows down the eastern coast of Greenland, but these are caught by another subartery of the Gulf Stream and sent back northwards into Baffin Bay. The only cold surface water which penetrates deeply into the Atlantic is that of the Labrador current, flowing from Baffin Bay to the waters around Newfoundland, and each spring carrying vast amounts of ice, as well as icebergs calved from the glaciers of Greenland and arctic Canada. The ice-choked and stormy Labrador Sea, and the floating mountains of glacial ice which wander down the eastern shores of Newfoundland each summer, pre-sented hazards unknown to the early navigators of western and northern Europe. The Labrador Current also brings arctic life forms — fish, seals, walrus, whales and polar bears — to Newfoundland coasts which lie as far south as the warm shores of western France.

The winds of the North Atlantic parallel the ocean currents over which they flow. The entire system circulates in a clockwise gyre around a high-pressure area, cen-tred over the Azores and extending westward across the Sargasso Sea. Around this high, the Trade Winds flow southward down the coasts of Portugal and North Africa, then swing westward towards South America and the Caribbean. Their northern counterparts are the Westerlies, flowing up the North American coast and then north-eastwards to the British Isles and Europe. To the north of the Wester-lies, in the latitudes of Norway and Iceland, is a weaker set of northerly and northeasterly winds composed of cold and heavy Arctic air, sinking and flowing southwards around a high-pressure area centred on the Greenland ice cap. These were the winds used by early northern navi-gators to reach Greenland and eastern Canada, in the same way that the Spanish used the Trade Winds to reach the Caribbean and South America. The eastbound voy-ages of both northerners and southerners depended on the Westerlies and the Gulf Stream to carry them back to Europe.

For early navigators, as for con-temporary pleasure sailors, the North Atlantic was essentially a summer sea. In winter, the temper-ature gradient between subtropical and Arctic air masses steepens. Consequently, the winds are stronger and more dangerous. Autumn hurricanes and tropical storms breed in the Carribean and whirl northwards, throwing destructive winds and massive waves across the fishing banks of eastern Canada and far out into the Atlantic. Winter darkness, ice, gales and freezing spray make the north-ern portions of the ocean a region to avoid from autumn until spring. The mediaeval Norse had rules against beginning an Atlantic voyage after September, and most other early voyagers soon learned to do likewise.

Yet despite constant threats of fog, drift-ice and storms, the summer Atlantic can bring long periods of fine weather. Under clear skies and a pleasant breeze, the long ocean swells roll endlessly toward a distant horizon. In north-ern regions the sky never darkens during summer nights, and the calm surface of the ocean is alive with whales, seals and seabirds. These were the conditions which, at some time well over 1,000 years ago, first tempted Europeans to pilot their fragile boats westward into the immensity of the North Atlantic.

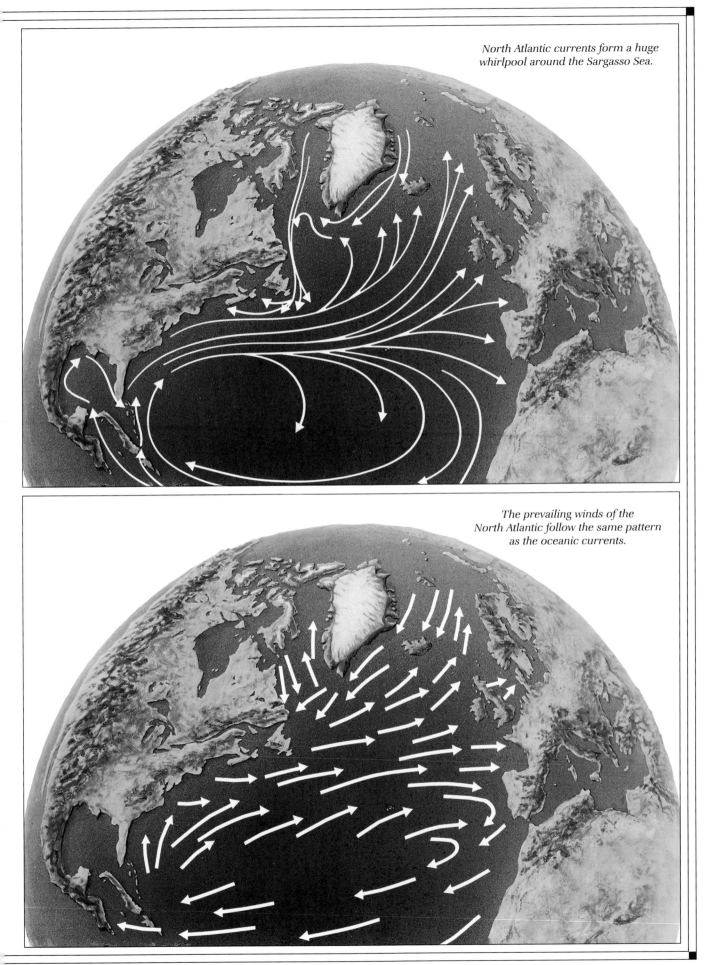

North Atlantic currents form a huge whirlpool around the Sargasso Sea.

The prevailing winds of the North Atlantic follow the same pattern as the oceanic currents.

undropping fair wind. A certain holy man informed me that in two summer days and the night between, sailing in a little boat of two thwarts, he came to land on one of them. Some of these islands are very small; nearly all of them are separated one from the other by narrow sounds. On these islands hermits who have sailed from our Scotia [another name for Ireland] have lived for roughly a hundred years. But, even as they have been constantly uninhabited since the world's beginning, so now, because of Norse pirates, they are empty of anchorites, but full of innumerable sheep and a great many different kinds of seafowl. I have never found these islands mentioned in the books of scholars.

This description most adequately fits the Faeroe Islands, located 200 kilometres northwest of the Shetlands and almost midway between Scotland and Iceland. Their name ("Faereyjar," Sheep Islands in Old Norse) is derived from the wild sheep found there by the early Norse settlers, which must have been left by the Irish hermits who had previously occupied the islands. The description is also reminiscent of St. Brendan's "Isle of Sheep" and "Isle of Birds."

It was without doubt the eruption of an Icelandic volcano, such as this, which is described in The Voyage of Saint Brendan: *"the whole mountain, right down to sea level, glowed like a pyre."*

Another of Dicuil's statements places Irish hermits even further to the north and west. Continuing his description of the North Atlantic islands, he reports on an island that lies six days' sail to the north of Britain:

It is now thirty years since priests who lived in that island from the first day of February to the first day of August told me that not only at the summer solstice, but in the days on either side of it, the setting sun hides itself at the evening hour as if behind a little hill, so that no darkness occurs during that brief period of time, but whatever task a man wishes to perform, even to picking the lice out of his shirt, he can manage it precisely as in broad daylight... They deal in fallacies who have written that the sea around the island is frozen, and that there is continous day without night from the vernal to the autumnal equinox, and vice versa, perpetual night from the autumnal equinox to the vernal; for those sailing at an expected time of great cold have made their way thereto, and dwelling on the island enjoyed always alternate night and day save at the time of the solstice. But after one day's sailing from there to the north they found the frozen sea.

This description can only apply to Iceland, which lies just below the Arctic Circle and thus falls just short of experiencing the midnight sun at midsummer. The ice conditions portrayed in this account also fit those of Iceland, the north coast of which lies close to the edge of the Arctic pack.

The "Papar" of Iceland

Dicuil's geographical treatise recounts that Irish monks had probably settled the Faeroe Islands shortly after A.D. 700, and that by A.D. 800 they had established at least seasonal occupation of Iceland. His work, that of a sober geographer, supports the suggestion that the earlier and much more fanciful accounts of St. Brendan's travels may not have been based entirely on fictional stories. Dicuil's descriptions, in turn, are confirmed by accounts from a non-Irish source: that of the early Norse settlers of Iceland. According to *Landnamabok*, the Icelandic Book of the Settlements written in the twelfth century and recounting the Norse settlement of Iceland after about A.D. 870:

Before Iceland was settled from Norway, there were men there whom the Norsemen style "papar." These were Christians, and people consider that they must have been from the British Isles, because there were found left behind them Irish books, bells, and croziers, and other things besides, from which it might be deduced that they were Vestmenn (Irishmen). It is recorded in English books that at that time there was trafficking to and fro between those countries.

The term "papar" is probably derived from the Latin "papa," referring to priests or monks. Further evidence of Irish occupation remains in the form of Icelandic placenames such as Papey and Papos. Such names are scattered around the southeastern coast of the island, the area where early voyagers from Ireland would most likely have landed. Yet archaeological work (some of it undertaken by Dr. Kristjan Eldjarn, an archaeologist who was also Prime Minister of Iceland) has not yet turned up any definite evidence of early Irish occupation of the island.

Islendingabok, another twelfth-century Icelandic history, goes on to say that the papar "went away because they were not prepared to live with heathen men." We can easily imagine the passionate exhortations, threats, and violent confrontations between holy Irish monks and the Norse followers of Thor and Frey, which lie hidden behind this simple and laconic statement.

This statement also leaves an important question unanswered. Where did the "papar" flee when Norse ships began to arrive, carrying heathen men and (perhaps more dangerously) heathen women intent on settling Iceland? Some may have returned to Ireland, but much of that country had already been colonized by the Norse, and a return to Ireland meant renouncing vows of hermetic solitude. The islands east of Iceland were already in the hands of Norse settlers, and only isolated skerries were left for a life of monastic seclusion. Some

How does one describe an iceberg seen for the first time? The narrative of St. Brendan's voyage tells of a column in the sea, the colour of silver, harder than marble and as clear as crystal.

CHAPTER 3

VINLAND

The Norse were the first Europeans known to have definitely landed in the New World, and to have established colonies there. The archaeological remains of one of their settlements have been found on Canada's eastern coast, and they seem to have made occasional visits to the country for at least three centuries.

The Viking warrior carried a round wooden shield
with a central boss of iron. Shields were sometimes ornamented
with decorative patterns of nails.

The search for Vikings in the New World began in 1837, when the Danish scholar Carl Christian Rafn published a volume which he called *Antiquitates Americanae*, "American Antiquities." In it he proposed that two traditional Icelandic sagas (known as Eirik the Red's Saga and The Greenlanders' Saga) were evidence that Viking-period Europeans had reached North America about A.D. 1000 — 500 years before Columbus. This was not the first time the suggestion had been made, but it was the first time that the idea caught the public imagination. The book was soon translated into English and French, and it set off a search for Norse relics throughout the New World. More than 150 years later, that search continues.

Like most scholarly hunts, this one turned up many false trails, and discovered much evidence which was either mistaken or enthusiastically misunderstood. Most scholarly pursuits are carried out within the confines of an academic discipline. The subject of the mediaval Norse in North America, however, refused to be

In 1936, a prospector convinced the Royal Ontario Museum that he had discovered a cache of Norse weapons on his mining claim near Beardmore in northwestern Ontario. Later investigations showed that the story was false: the weapons are genuine, but they were brought from Norway during the present century.

confined in this way. Instead, it was a scholarly endeavour played out largely in the public press, and in which any discovery, or claim of discovery, found an avid public audience.

Why was there such great public interest in a mediaeval Norse presence in the New World? Enthusiasm for the subject is almost certainly related to the fact that, for the past 150 years, most North Americans have been immigrants from Europe or the descendants of recent immigrants. The discovery of an ancient European heritage in North America was interesting to people of recent European ancestry because it gave them a historical stake in the country: it helped people to feel at home among the alien forests and prairies that were so different from the settled homelands of their Old World ancestors.

Whatever the reason, several generations of North Americans have been fascinated with Viking exploration in the New World. To feed this fascination, hundreds of books and articles have been written, by individuals ranging from scholars through crackpots to confidence artists. The historical and literary evidence on the subject is very limited. There are, after all, only two legendary stories and a few vague references in other ancient texts. Archaeology, therefore, has been the main field of contention.

Spurious Evidence

Among the most famous archaeological finds associated with the search is a well-built stone tower near Newport, Rhode Island, which for over a century has been interpreted by some as a Viking fortress. Archaeological excavation around the base of the tower has shown that the structure was not Norse, and was undoubtedly built in the Colonial period; there are

This stone tower in Newport, Rhode Island, was built by early English colonists during the seventeenth century. Its construction fits well into colonial American building traditions, and bears no resemblance to mediaeval Scandinavian structures.

even historical accounts in which the governor of Rhode Island at the time refers to it as "my stone-built mill." Nevertheless, the "Newport Tower" is still proposed by enthusiasts as evidence of a Norse presence in the New World.

A much more specific piece of evidence was turned up in Minnesota near the end of the last century. This is a stone slab covered in runic writing, telling of a fourteenth-century Norse expedition to the area. The stone was said to have been found by a Swedish immigrant farmer, beneath the roots of a large tree. It was immediately denounced as an obvious forgery,

and a bad one at that: the runes were in two or three different styles, and the grammar and language were that of nineteenth-century Scandinavia, rather than of fourteenth-century Iceland. Nevertheless, the "Kensington Stone" now has its own museum.

The Kensington Stone has also spawned finds of several other runic stones: one appeared in Maine a few years ago, but turned out to have been carved by someone whose only knowledge of runic writing came from studying the original fraudulent Kensington Stone. Other runic inscriptions have been found as far west as Oklahoma, and as far south as Paraguay. Scholars of Old Norse have denounced all of them as fakes.

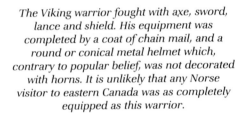

The Viking warrior fought with axe, sword, lance and shield. His equipment was completed by a coat of chain mail, and a round or conical metal helmet which, contrary to popular belief, was not decorated with horns. It is unlikely that any Norse visitor to eastern Canada was as completely equipped as this warrior.

The war-axe and heavy sword were the favoured weapons of Viking warriors. Besides smashing an enemy's shield, armour or bones, the axe also served as a multi-purpose tool in hunting, travelling and working wood.

Canada's unique contributions to the search are the "Beardmore Relics," a genuine and ancient Norse sword, axe and bell which were maintained to have been found on a mining claim north of Lake Superior during the 1930s. The specimens were purchased by the Royal Ontario Museum in Toronto. Closer investigation showed that they had been brought to Canada in 1923 by a young Norwegian immigrant whose father had been a collector of antiquities, and who had later used them as security for a loan.

Most of the other archaeological evidence that has turned up has been equally misinterpreted. Iron battle-axes of an apparently Viking form keep appearing, but turn out to be the blades of nineteenth-century tobacco-cutters. Holes drilled in rocks by nineteenth-century farmers, into which they poured black powder to blast the rocks, are interpreted as holes drilled by Viking sailors, into which they drove iron pegs in order to moor their ships — a technique never employed in the Old World.

A generation ago, the scholarly search for New World Vikings appeared to have reached an impasse. Few scholars, were willing to join the hunt, afraid of sullying their reputations by associating with the long record of fraud and misinterpretation which had accumulated. No genuine archaeological evidence had been recovered in over a century of searching. The few literary and historical records appeared to be mined out; all useful information in the Norse sagas had long ago been recognized, leaving only quibbles over the interpretations of unclear terms and vague geographical descriptions. Mid-twentieth-century scholars knew little more about the subject than had Professor Rafn in 1837, and increasingly, were divided into two camps. In one camp were enthusiasts who believed in most of the fraudulent archaeological evidence, and who pictured bands of courageous Vikings exploring and even settling much of North America. In the other were those who considered the sagas to be fantastic stories, or to reflect, at most, a brief Norse foray to the eastern coast of the continent.

The past thirty years, however, have produced a new wave of archaeological discovery, which has validated the literary evidence and brought new respect to the search for Vikings. It now seems certain that the mediaeval Norse did reach eastern North America, and that they may have visited portions of the area over a period of several centuries. Before examining this evidence, here is a brief look at the background to the Norse venture in the New World.

The Viking Age

During the ninth and tenth centuries A.D., most of Christian Europe became painfully aware of their heathen Scandinavian neighbours to the north. The beginning of Viking expansion is generally marked by the sacking in A.D. 793 of the monastery at Lindisfarne, in northeastern England, and of the holy island of Iona two years later. During the following cen-

For 300 years, from the eighth to the tenth centuries, the Viking Norse travelled and occupied countries further and further from their homelands. While Danes and Norwegians pillaged the coasts of western Europe and even North Africa, the Swedes founded a kingdom in Russia and threatened Constantinople. Their merchants regularly travelled as far as Baghdad. At the same time, Norwegians expanded westward across the North Atlantic to Iceland, Greenland and eastern Canada.

41

tury, the isolated groups of Viking raiders gradually developed into Norse armies, who seized and occupied large areas of Western Europe. In the east, Norse adventurers settled the river valleys of Russia, exploring and trading as far as the Black Sea and Constantinople. But by the late ninth century, events had begun to go badly for the Norse: there were military defeats in Europe, while at home King Harald Fairhair was suppressing the powers of individual Norse chiefs in an attempt to unify Norway.

For many of these chiefs, the best solution to their problems lay in leaving home in order to

This eleventh-century carving in antler, representing the head of a warrior, is only 5 cm high.

At L'Anse aux Meadows, on the northern tip of Newfoundland, lies evidence of an early attempt to establish a European colony in America. This scene depicts the arrival of Norse settlers at the site: the colonists are sheltered in tents, while the men cut turf for the construction of permanent houses.

seek land elsewhere. During the ninth century, the most attractive land lay in the almost uninhabited islands of the North Atlantic. For decades the Norse had occupied the Celtic portions of the British Isles, living and intermarrying with the local people. Here they must have learned of the islands discovered by Irish monks, who for centuries had taken to the sea in their skin-covered curraghs, seeking solitude and the absence of temptation, far from the haunts of men. As noted in the previous chapter, such monks had established small monastic communities on the Shetlands, Orkneys and Faeroes, and by A.D. 800 were occupying Iceland, at least during the summer months. Their isolation would not last long, as Norse settlers followed in their path. When the Norse reached Iceland about A.D. 860, they recounted that they had displaced prior occupants of the country, who left behind religious books and other objects showing them to have been Irish.

During the "settlement period" of Iceland, between about A.D. 870 and 930, immigrants flocked to the island, which had an estimated population of 30,000 people by the end of the period. All useful land had been taken, and adventurers or fighters who could no longer get along with their neighbours began to look elsewhere. Eirik the Red's exploration of Greenland about A.D. 980 arose from such circumstances. The immigrants who followed him to establish colonies on the southwestern coast of Greenland soon swelled the population to an estimated 3,000 people.

Canada Discovered

For the next four centuries ships from Greenland, Iceland and northern Europe plied the North Atlantic, bringing immigrants, taking people on visits to the Old Country and, most importantly, pursuing the trade upon which the Greenland colonies depended for a livelihood. The Greenland settlements were only 800 kilometres from the Labrador coast of North America, and less then 500 kilometres, little more than two days' sailing, from Baffin Island. The

When Eirik the Red explored Greenland, he found remains of earlier occupation, but no living occupants of the newly discovered country. This situation would not last long; for at the same time that Eirik's followers were colonizing southwestern Greenland, the ancestors of the Inuit were pushing eastward from Alaska. The Inuit were an Alaskan people who, on the margins of iron-age Asia, had developed a sophisticated maritime hunting way of life based on the use of skin-covered boats: the single-man kayak, and the large umiak capable of transporting an entire camp or serving as a platform from which to hunt animals as large as whales. The early Inuit were great whalers, and this prey supplied them with enormous stores of meat, and oil for use as fuel.

The early Inuit spread rapidly eastward across the Canadian Arctic, displacing earlier occupants of the area. By as early as the twelfth century A.D., they had crossed from Ellesmere Island to occupy northwestern Greenland, then began to spread southward towards the areas occupied by the Norse. It was inevitable that the two immigrant groups would meet, but there is no historical reference to such contact until 1266, when a report states that a Norse hunting party in the Disko Bay area of western Greenland had found traces of natives. Another source, probably dating from about the same period, states that in the north the hunters had discovered small people whom they called "Skraelings," who had no iron but used stone knives and weapons of walrus ivory. As the Inuit expanded southward down the Greenland coast, they must have come into increasingly frequent contact with the Norse settlers but Norse historical documents are almost silent on the subject of meetings with the Inuit.

Norse Accounts of the Inuit

One account, dating from about A.D. 1350, states that the Western Settlement (the more northerly of the two Norse colonies) had been abandoned and was in the hands of the Skraelings. A second indicates that in about 1418, the Eastern Settlement had been attacked "from the nearby shores of the heathens," and that most of the churches had been burned. The general impression given by the Norse accounts is one of infrequent and hostile contact between the two groups, eventually leading to the destruc-

The remains of the church at Hvalsey, in the Eastern Settlement of Norse Greenland. This thirteenth-century building is the best preserved Norse Greenlandic structure.

Archaeologists found this portion of
a bronze balance in an Inuit village on western
Ellesmere Island. Such objects were
used by Norse traders for weighing coins
and other small objects.

Schledermann in eastern Ellesmere Island yielded pieces of woollen cloth, chain mail, and fragments of coopered barrels or tubs of oak. A portion of a bronze bowl came from a site I excavated on Devon Island. All of this material must have been obtained by the Inuit from the Norse, either through trading or through more hostile contacts. Many of the Inuit villages containing this material appear to date from the twelfth or early thirteenth centuries, suggesting that contact between the groups occurred con-

tion of the Norse colonies. There is only one brief story which does not tell of hostilities: in 1385 Bjorn Einarsson, named "Jerusalem-farer" because he had made a pilgrimage to the Holy Land, was storm-driven to Greenland, where he rescued a Skraeling boy and girl from a rock in the sea. The children lived with him as faithful servants, and killed themselves when he departed for Iceland two years later.

Archaeological evidence accumulated over the past decade sketches a distinctly different picture, one which suggests that we should perhaps not place too much faith in the historical documents of the period. Many of the early Inuit winter villages that have been excavated in the eastern Arctic have produced fragments of smelted metal, and those excavated by Peter

The Greenlandic Norse maintained sufficient contact with Europe to follow clothing styles. Homespun woollen clothing which has been found in excavations, notably in the cemetery at Herjolfsness, is similar in style to that worn by fourteenth-century Europeans.

This type of hood, with a long ornamental tail, was very popular in Europe. The specimen was excavated from the graveyard at Herjolfsness.

siderably earlier than reported by the Norse. This interpretation is supported by the description of a people who can only be Inuit, in a geographical account written by an Arabic scholar about A.D. 1150.

An Arabic Description of the Inuit?

Al-Idrisi is the respected author of a well-known mediaeval treatise on world geography entitled *Nuzhat al-Mushtaq*. In his description of the North Atlantic Ocean, he states:

There are also sea animals of such enormous size that the inhabitants of the inner isles use their bones and vertebrae in place of wood in

The Norse established two colonies on the portion of Greenland's west coast which lay beyond the inland ice-sheet (1 and 2). Their first encounters with Inuit occurred further north on the west coast (3).

In the year 986, Eirik the Red founded the Norse colony on the southwest coast of Greenland. Within a few years, turf-built farms were scattered along the fiord coasts where the Norse hunted, fished, and raised sheep and cattle. It was from such a farm that the sagas tell of Leif, the son of Eirik, departing to search for Vinland.

constructing houses. They also use them for making clubs, darts, lances, knives, seats, ladders, and in general, all things which elsewhere are made from wood.

If we interpret the large animals as whales, and the "inner isles" as those deepest in the North Atlantic, this description may well refer to the early Inuit, who used whale bones as frames for their winter houses, as well as for many other artifacts. It is difficult to think of another North Atlantic population of the period who would fit this description. We might speculate that such a description could have reached northern Europe from Greenland, and been transferred to Sicily through the medium of the Norman occupation of the island. If so, this description would tend to confirm archaeological evidence from Arctic Canada, which indicates that contact between Inuit and Norse was occurring at least a century earlier than was reported in Norse historical documents.

Norse Traders?

What would have been the nature of these early and unrecorded contacts? The widespread distribution of smelted iron, copper and bronze on Canadian Arctic Inuit sites suggests that metal, even in small fragments, was a valuable trade commodity to the early Inuit, and was widely distributed through Inuit trade routes. The Vinland sagas indicate that the Norse were willing to trade with the Skraelings, and it seems likely that trade with the Inuit would have been very beneficial to the Norse. The Greenland colonies depended on trade with Europe for many of their requirements — grain, metal, timber, and luxury goods such as bishop's vestments. Furthermore, after 1261 they were required to pay fines and an annual tribute to the Norwegian king, as well as tithes and crusade taxes to the Roman church. This tribute was paid in the products of the country — primarily walrus and narwhal ivory, but also in walrus hides, polar-bear skins and, on at least one occasion, a live polar bear.

Walrus are ice-loving animals, and are no longer found in the subarctic region of Green-

ing, fishing and hunting for food. Yet such was the importance of European trade that the *Nordrsetur* hunt was an integral part of the Norse Greenlanders' way of life. The early Inuit who had occupied Arctic Canada and northwestern Greenland by about A.D. 1100, possessed quantities of ivory, as can be seen from the archaeological remains of their settlements. If they were willing to trade ivory for small scraps of metal and worn-out tools, as were their descendants of the seventeenth and eighteenth centuries, it would have been profitable for the Norse to have exploited this trade. Is there any evidence that such trade did actually occur?

It is impossible to answer this question on the basis of the sparse archaeological evidence available. However, two finds from early Inuit villages in Arctic Canada could be significant. The first, found by Patricia Sutherland in the northwestern part of Ellesmere Island, is the beam of a folding bronze balance, similar to those used by Norse traders for weighing coins and other small objects. This characteristic trader's tool, the only one known to have been found west of Iceland, and discovered in an Inuit village 2,000 kilometres from the Greenlandic Norse colonies, hints at the existence of some form of trade between Norse and Inuit.

The second object, found by Deborah Sabo in a thirteenth-century village on the south coast of Baffin Island, suggests the actual presence of Norsemen in Arctic Canada at that time.

land where the Norse colonies were located. During the relatively warm climatic period when the Norse colonies were occupied, walrus may have been scarce and easily exterminated in southwestern Greenland. In order to obtain ivory, Norse hunters had to travel at least 400 kilometres north of the settlements to the area known as the *Nordrsetur*, the northern hunting grounds. Such hunts must have put great pressure on the Norse economy, depriving the colonies of manpower needed for farm-

It is a small wooden figurine carved in typically Inuit style, with a flat, featureless face and stumpy arms; it is unusual, however, in showing an individual dressed in a long gown or robe, with what appears to be a cross on the chest. The clothing is consistent with European clothing of the time. Baffin Island Inuit could not have crossed Davis Strait to see Norse Greenlanders dressed in this fashion, and it is very unlikely that the figurine was traded from Greenlandic Inuit, who had a much different tradition in carving figurines representing Europeans. The Baffin Island figurine seems most likely to have been made locally by someone who had seen a Norse Greenlander, perhaps on Baffin Island or in Labrador.

Baffin Island, the Helluland of the sagas, was known to the Norse, and the Norse may have coasted it for some 300 years on their voyages to the forests of Markland. It seems likely that at least occasional landings were made, and that there was contact with the Inuit occupants of the region. From such contacts, a sporadic and opportunistic trading relationship may have been established, one that may have served as the basis for a relationship between the Norse Greenlanders and the Inuit who eventually moved into southwestern Greenland.

Norse-Inuit Relations in Greenland

Relations between Norse and Inuit in Greenland must have been considerably more intense than with the peoples encountered during voyages along the fringes of Arctic Canada, and more intense and complex than suggested by the rare Norse historical records which mention contact with Inuit. Recent archaeological work has shown that the Inuit had advanced down the coast of western Greenland considerably earlier than had been generally thought. Radiocarbon dates now suggest that the Inuit had settled the Disko Bay area as early as the thirteenth century, well before the Norse accounts first mention encounters with Skraelings in the north. By the next century, Inuit had occupied the outer coastal regions of southwestern Greenland, while Norse farms lined the shores of interior fiords. For the following one or two centuries substantial populations of

This watercolour was painted by the nineteenth-century Greenlandic artist Aaron of Kangeq. It illustrates an Inuit legend telling of the first meeting of Inuit with the Norse.

Later Voyagers to Greenland?

The last known visitors to report on the state of the Norse colonies in Greenland were the crew of an Icelandic ship that was storm-driven to Greenland in 1406 and stayed for four years. Between that time and the rediscovery of Greenland by the Portuguese around 1500, there is almost a century of silence, during which the Norse colonies disappeared. Yet a few names emerge from vague or casual sixteenth-century references, which hint at fifteenth-century voyages into the far northwestern Atlantic.

Several sources mention a pair of northern mariners named Pining and Pothorst, who are said to have undertaken mysterious business in the northwestern Atlantic during the later fifteenth century. We meet Didrik Pining elsewhere (see "The Newe Found Islande"), as the governor of Iceland who brought a temporary halt to British piracy in that country during the 1480s. Pining and his companion Pothorst were probably either Danish or German, and the pair do not seem to have been above piracy themselves. Several accounts describe them setting up a great "sea-mark" on an island or rock named Hvitsark, located somewhere west of Iceland. This structure is said to have been built either to warn mariners against the local pirates who attacked in small ships without keels (Inuit kayakers?), or as a guide to serve Pining and Pothorst in their own piratical endeavours. Hvitsark ("White Shirt") was probably the Icelandic name for a large glacier on the east coast of Greenland,

and the stories seem to derive from the fact that Pining and Pothorst undertook one or more voyages to Greenland during the late fifteenth century. We may assume either that they were engaged in unrecorded trade with Norse Greenland, or that they were raiding the isolated farmsteads of the dying colonies.

A few vague sixteenth-century accounts also make reference to a man named Johannes Scolvus, a Latin version of a name which has been interpreted as referring to a Dane or Norwegian (Jon Scolp), a Swede (Jon Scolvsen), a Welshman (John Lloyd) or a Pole (Jan Kolnus). Scolvus' name is usually associated with the general area of Labrador, Baffin Island and Hudson Strait, and with a voyage which took place in 1476. It is possible, as some scholars have suggested (without supplying anything like proof), that Scolvus may have been linked with the Pining-Pothorst endeavours in the area.

Another name, and another European nation, is also mentioned by sixteenth-century documents purporting to tell of fifteenth-century explorations in the northwest. Some of the maps that mention Johannes Scolvus associate him with a waterway to the west of Greenland labelled the "Strait of the Three Brothers." The three brothers are generally taken to be the brothers Corte-Real — Gaspar, Miguel and Vasqueanes— the Azoreans who made voyages to Greenland, Labrador and Newfoundland about A.D. 1500, and whose name may have been attached to either

Davis Strait (between Greenland and Baffin Island) or Hudson Strait (between Baffin Island and Labrador). But by the late 1500s the name Corte-Real also began to be mentioned in connection with an earlier discovery of New World territories. This discovery was said to have been made by the father of the better-known explorers, an Azorean governor named Joao Vaz Corte-Real. A few authors have even linked him with the Pining-Pothorst-Scolvus team, suggesting that all four sailed as an international brigade to explore the New World Arctic.

As discussed elsewhere (see "The Labrador"), it is quite possible that Portuguese or Portuguese-Azoreans did make discoveries in the northwest Atlantic some time before Columbus' voyage. Yet the evidence for such discoveries is vague, and certainly not sufficient to be ascribed to any individual whose name is first mentioned over a century after his reputed voyage. Nevertheless, Joao Vaz Corte-Real is considered by many contemporary Portuguese as the discoverer of the New World. As an Azorean official with interests in exploration, he may well have been in a position to undertake voyages in the northwestern Atlantic. Yet until more precise evidence is unearthed by historians, Joao Vaz Corte-Real must take his place with Pining, Pothorst and Johannes Scolvus, as merely a possible voyager to the New World.

The stories linking all these names with fifteenth-century discoveries in the northwest Atlantic may imply, however, that the apparent break in communication between Europe and Norse Greenland may have been less complete than is generally believed. Although few Icelandic vessels travelled to Greenland in the fifteenth century, their place may have been taken by Danes, Germans, English and Portuguese. These voyagers may have been the authors of the piratical raids on the farms of Norse Greenland that are described in Greenlandic Inuit legends. They also may have been the agency through which European navigators continued to be aware of lands in the distant northwestern Atlantic.

This statue of Gaspar Corte-Real stands in front of the Newfoundland and Labrador legislature in St. John's.

Norse and Inuit lived in this region, and it seems inevitable that they must have worked out some means of sharing the country and its resources. Whatever their relationships, they must have been more complex than the simple animosity referred to in the historical records.

Archaeology has so far been unable to suggest the nature of this set of relationships. One recent find, however, offers an intriguing hint. Recent excavations by Claus Andreason of the Greenland Museum at a Norse farm called Nipaitsoq in the Western Settlement, recovered a number of iron knife blades, made in characteristic Norse form. Among them are blades made not from smelted iron, but from meteoric iron. This material almost certainly came from the iron meteorites of the Cape York District in far northwestern Greenland, a source in the heart of Inuit territory and one that had been used by the Inuit for centuries. Is it possible, then, that there was not only trade between Norse and Inuit, but that this trade was not simply an exchange of European manufactured goods for native raw materials? The Norse Greenlanders must have been chronically short of iron, and the Inuit had access to meteoric iron. In fact, a trade in metal may have passed both ways between the two groups.

Inuit History

Other hints of close and complex relationships between the two cultures comes from the oral history of the Greenlandic Inuit. When the Danish missionary Niels Egede reached Greenland in 1769, he was told stories which indicated that the Inuit and the Norse had traded, and had eventually been on relatively good terms. When the Norse were attacked from the sea, Inuit stories told of the Inuit taking Norse women and children to the inner fiords for their protection. Legends collected by the administrator and folklorist Hinrich Rink in the mid-nineteenth century, while more complete, are suspect in that they came from Inuit who had been in contact with Scandinavians for a century. These legends centre on the story of Ungortok, a chief of the Norsemen. It is a complex tale of violence resulting in the destruction of a Norse farmstead. The various versions, however, include stories of an Inuit girl working as a servant on a Norse farm (a transformation of the more general Inuit story of Navaranak, a girl who is captured by Indians), and of a Norseman and an Inuk who were best friends and who had friendly archery contests. Such relationships must have been at least conceivable to the people who built the story of Ungortok.

Interestingly, an Icelandic version of the Ungortok story, collected a few decades before the Inuit version was collected and published by Rink, has recently been recognized. The Norse chieftain at the centre of this story is named Ingjaldur (whom the Inuit call Ingjalli). Linguists inform me that Ingjaldur, or Ingjalli, can easily be transformed into the Inuttituut name Ungortok (meaning "he who is stubborn"). The Icelandic story also contains two Inuit words, *innuk* and *kayak*, and an Inuit placename, *Nabaitsoq*, which may be identical with the Nipaitsoq mentioned earlier as the Norse farm that produced blades of meteoric iron. Using different placenames, both the Icelandic and Inuit versions place the action at a locality near the head of Ameralik Fiord in the old Western Settlement of the Norse. Considering the low level of communication between Greenland and Iceland from mediaeval times to the nineteenth century, the evidence suggests that we may have here two versions of a shared historical tradition. If this is true, it would lead to a radical reassessment of relationships between the Inuit and Mediaeval Norse in Greenland.

Disappearance of the Greenlandic Norse

When the Norse Greenlandic colonies died out, probably about the time that Cabot, Cortereal and Cartier were re-establishing contact between Europe and the eastern coast of Canada, it was almost certainly not because of attacks by the Inuit, among whom they had lived for several generations. Their decline and eventual disappearance probably resulted more from a deteriorating climate, combined with a rapid decline in the value of their commercial products. With the growth of Hanseatic trade in the east and Portuguese exploration in Africa, furs and ivory began to reach Europe from other sources, and the Greenlandic trade lost much of its historic value. Greenlandic life must have stayed relatively constant, while Europe was undergoing the immense social changes required to take it from feudalism to mercantile capitalism.

Abandoned by their Norse king and their Roman church, neither of whom any longer bothered to send ships to Greenland, and increasingly harassed by European pirates, the

Norse colonies were more likely the victims of economic forces than of native attacks. It was a sad end to a heroic venture that had begun with the European discovery of North America.

Greenlandic Inuit posed in their kayaks for this photograph, taken around 1900.

ern boundary is very vague; but the east coast is marked by two deep inlets. A label identifies this island as *Vinilanda Insula* (Island of Vinland). This caused the scholars even greater concern. Although Vinland, the land discovered by the medieval Greenlandic Norse around A.D. 1000, was generally considered to be eastern North America, and although its name appears in European geographies from the eleventh century and later, it had never appeared on a map dating from the period before Columbus' voyages.

The Map is Tested

Knowing that the map might represent a major advance in knowledge of mediaeval European geography, but aware too that they would be judged extremely gullible should the map prove to be a forgery, the Yale scholars set to work to authenticate their find. First, they satisfied themselves that the *Tartar Relation* manuscript was a genuine early fifteenth-century document. This was accomplished fairly easily, and most critics do not doubt its authenticity. Then they compared the Old World portions of the Vinland Map with other known maps of the period, and were satisfied that its style fitted the period from which it was purported to come the only unexpected elements: were the Greenland and Vinland configurations and their accompanying notes. The scholars analyzed the handwriting of both the *Tartar Relation* and the Vinland Map. Both appeared to be in the same hand and in a style characteristic of the Upper Rhineland during the early fifteenth century. Next, they checked the watermarks of the paper on which the *Tartar Relation* was written: it came from a small paper-mill in southern Germany or Switzerland, and also dated to the early fifteenth century.

The map itself, however, was drawn on parchment, a writing material made from animal skin, which of course lacks watermarks and could not be so easily dated. There was, though, one simple way to check whether the questionable Map and the apparently genuine *Tartar Relation* belonged together. Both documents contained several tiny holes made by book-worms which, at some point in its history, had tunnelled through the volume. Unfortunately, the worm holes in the map did not align with those in the *Tartar Relation* manuscript, suggesting that the two documents had been bound together only recently, and casting further doubt on the map's authenticity.

Then something very curious happened. Yale had first been approached by the American bookdealer who owned the volume containing the Vinland Map and *Tartar Relation* in 1957. In 1958, one of the Yale scholars who had shown polite interest in the volume happened to look through an English book-dealer's catalogue, where he saw a copy of a fairly common late-mediaeval manuscript, the *Speculum Historiale* written by Vincent de Beauvais, selling for a low price. He ordered it for his own collection, and when it arrived he lent it to the book dealer who had approached him earlier. That evening, the scholar received a telephone call from the dealer, who had compared the Beauvais manuscript with the *Tartar Relation*: the handwriting was the same, the paper was the same, and when the Speculum volume was placed between the Map and the *Relation*, the worm-holes all aligned! It seemed that all three manuscripts had originally been bound together for a long time, and had been separated only recently. The supposition was that both volumes came onto the market at about the same time, from the same private library, where they had become separated at some time during the past century when the original bindings had worn out and new ones had been added to the Map and the *Relation*. The original bindings remained with the *Speculum* manuscript, and were in a style consistent with the handwriting and the paper of the *Tartar Relation*: from southern Germany or Switzerland in the fifteenth century.

Thus, after an apparently amazing coincidence and several years of study, the Yale scholars finally concluded that the Vinland Map was a genuine fifteenth-century depiction of the world, which also showed a portion of North America. They even suggested that it may have been drawn at the Council of Basel (A.D. 1431-49), an important church event that had attracted scholars from all over Europe and could have served as a centre for the exchange of geographical and historical knowledge.

Not everyone was convinced by the Yale scholarship. The critics, who continued to suggest that the map was most probably a recent forgery inserted into an old manuscript, were especially suspicious of the representation of Greenland. The true outline of Greenland was

Martin Beheim constructed his globe in Germany in 1492, the year of Columbus' first voyage (pictured here is a facsimile made in 1847). It illustrates a view of the world which convinced Columbus of the feasibility of reaching the Indies by sailing westwards from Europe. On his way to the Orient, Columbus hoped to find two landfalls: first, the mythical island of Antillia (near the sailing ship in the centre of the picture), and then Cipangu (Japan).

not known to European scholarship before the early twentieth century, and this supposedly fifteenth-century representation was simply too accurate. Others were troubled by the Latin used in the legends on the map. Scientists at the British Museum briefly examined the map in 1967, and while their results were not conclusive, there were indications that the parchment on which the map was drawn might have been chemically treated, perhaps in order to remove an older document and substitute a recently-drawn map. The Vinland Map remained in a sort of scholarly limbo for over a decade. Its authenticity was simply not certain enough to prove that Europe had geographical knowledge of North America half a century before the voyages of Columbus.

A Forgery!

The final blow came in 1974, when a Chicago laboratory specializing in the chemical analysis of very small samples was allowed to remove several tiny scraps of ink from the map, and subject them to chemical and microscopic tests. These showed that the ink contained 30 percent of a form of titanium dioxide, a major constituent of twentieth-century white paints and products such as the white erasing fluid used by typists, which had not been available before about 1920. It was suggested that a forger had used titanium-based paint to artificially age the lines he had drawn in a strong black modern ink. Critics of the Vinland Map were triumphant, while its supporters were chastened by the demonstration that fine schol-

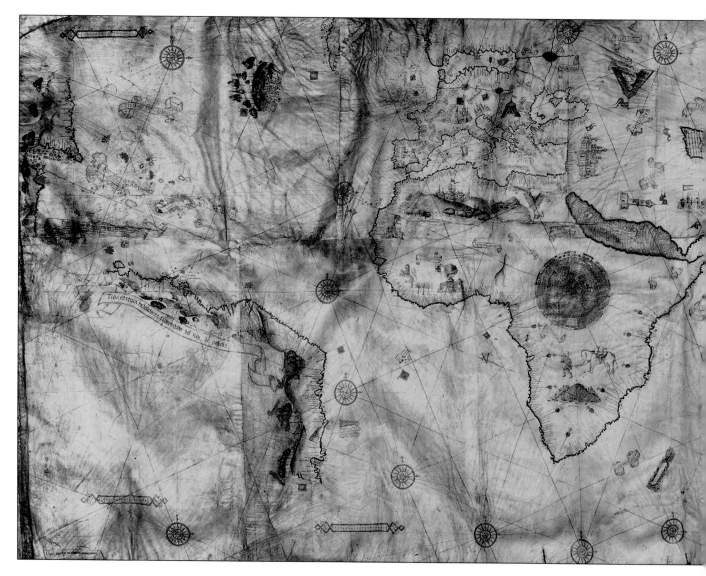

A map drawn about 1502 by the Genoese cartographer Nicolo de Caverio. The semicircular island covered with tall trees represents the Newfoundland and Labrador coasts explored by the Portuguese Gaspar Corte-Real. The shape of this configuration resembles that of Vinland on the Vinland Map.

ars could be duped by a clever forger. Through a series of vague inferences, the forgery began to be attributed to an obscure Yugoslavian church scholar, an enthusiast of mediaeval missionaries, who would have had access to the necessary knowledge and materials before his death in 1924.

Little was heard of the Vinland Map over the next decade. Most scholars who referred to it did so only to remark it as an obvious fraud. Yet some people continued to be troubled by two questions, both essentially psychological in nature. First, the alleged forger must have gone to great trouble to find an ancient parchment which could be associated by worm-holes with genuine fifteenth-century documents, and he had been extremely careful to match the handwriting and contents of the map with the associated documents. Would such a forger then have used a patently twentieth-century ink when a perfectly good mediaeval ink could have been easily made at home from such ingredients as acorns and soot? Second, why would a twentieth-century forger of such a map draw a modern likeness of Greenland? Surely this would be a certain give away. Any competent forger would represent Greenland either as a vague blob in the northwestern Atlantic, or as a peninsula depending from a polar continent, as it was shown on other fifteenth-century maps.

Vindication: 1986

In early 1986, the fortunes of the Vinland Map changed once again. Physicists at the

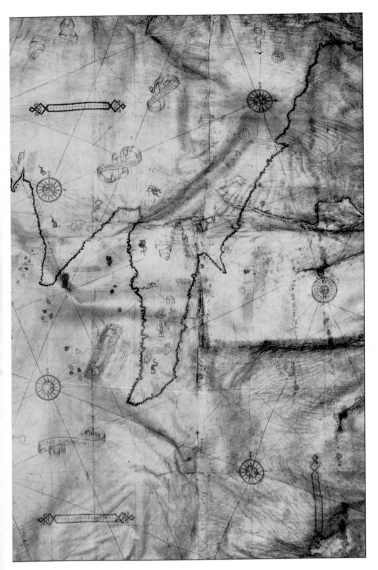

University of California had developed non-destructive techniques for studying the chemical characteristics of ancient documents. Sub-atomic particles, accelerated to immense speeds in a cyclotron, were aimed at a document in their path, and the resulting scatter of X-rays was measured in order to determine the number and amounts of chemicals in ancient paper and ink. The physicists had already tested the Dead Sea Scrolls and other documents, and were confident that their techniques gave accurate readings. This was much more sophisticated than the earlier Chicago tests on the ink of the Vinland Map. The only tests then available had required the destruction of the objects tested, so they had been based on tiny samples of ink, with the results extrapolated to the entire map. The accelerator tests were non-destructive, gave more accurate readings, and could be applied to the entire document. The California physicists declared that they had found only trace amounts of titanium in the ink

of the map, and that both ink and parchment were entirely characteristic of a fifteenth-century document. Suddenly, the Vinland Map was respectable again.

Significance of the Map

If the Vinland Map does prove to be a genuine fifteenth-century document, how can we explain its Greenland and Vinland configurations? The manner in which Greenland is represented is perhaps not as surprising as was thought when the map first came to light. The Greenland configuration is much less accurate than it first appears: the island is far too small in relation to the remainder of the map, and its north coast much further south than it should be. The coast has many apparently random indentations which cannot be matched with known bays and fiords. Only three features obviously coincide with modern maps: Greenland is represented as an island; the southern tip of the island is tapered in shape; and a long, straight section of the northwestern coast appears to represent Melville Bay.

During the early years of Norse settlement in Greenland, the climate was somewhat warmer than at present, and the amount of sea ice was probably considerably less than normal twentieth-century conditions. The standard sailing route from Iceland took ships directly west to a point on the East Greenland coast, then south to round Cape Farewell and north along the west coast to the settlements. Approximately the southern quarter of the east coast of Greenland was therefore well known, and it was probably assumed that the east and west coasts converged and met at Cape Farewell to form a tapered configuration. Archaeological finds reveal that Norse hunting expeditions penetrated as far north as the present Upernavik District, well over halfway up the western coast of the island and at the southern edge of Melville Bay; the straight and glaciered coast to the north was, therefore, probably within the geographical knowledge of the Norse.

But could the Norse have known that Greenland was an island? In the 1960s, when the map was first studied, it was generally thought that the Greenlandic Norse had had few if any contacts with the Inuit who arrived in Greenland at about the same time, and that such contacts would have been limited to hos-

Europe and encouraged eastern ventures by merchants such as the Polo family of Venice. Europeans were travelling farther and more frequently, and they increasingly needed clear instructions on how to reach one place from another without running onto a dangerous coast or island on the way. Cartographers began to provide these instructions in graphic form. Early mapmakers had very little knowledge to work with, however, and that knowledge was mostly in the form of old writings and more recent travellers' tales. The information available to these cartographers told of an Atlantic Ocean sprinkled with islands of various shapes and sizes, and their maps reflected these ideas.

The fifteenth century saw a rapid increase in the production of maps and nautical charts. It also saw an increased number of Atlantic islands marked on these charts, as well as a certain standardization of the names, shapes and locations of these islands. Islands such as "St. Brendan's," "Brasil," and "Antilia" or "Seven Cities," began to be noted by most European cartographers. "St. Brendan's Isle" had its legendary origin in Dark Age explorations by Irish monks, and was usually placed far to the west of Ireland. The island of "Brasil" or "Hy-Brasil" has a more obscure derivation, probably as an enchanted island in Irish folklore; it appears on many maps drawn after A.D. 1325, usually to the west of Ireland and in association with St. Brendan's Isle. The *Itineraries*, written about 1480 by the Englishman William Worcestre, give sailing directions for "he who wishes to sail to the island of Brasyle," advising him to set his course from the Blasket Islands off the west coast of Ireland.

To the south, the largest Atlantic island was known as "Antilia" or the "Isle of Seven Cities." It usually appears on fifteenth-century maps as a large rectangular island, with or without the place names of its cities. According to legend, it had been discovered and settled by seven bishops who had fled Portugal with their congregations following the eighth century Moorish invasion. Columbus believed in the existence of Antilia, and seems to have looked for it as a convenient staging post on the western route to Asia. He knew of a report that a fifteenth-century Portuguese ship had been storm-driven to this island, had been well received by Portuguese-speaking inhabitants, and had found grains of gold in the sand which they loaded

aboard for use in their cook-box. He also seems to have been impressed by the calculations of the Florentine cosmographer Paolo Toscanelli, who stated in 1474 that only 50 degrees of longitude separated Antilia from "Cipangu," the name by which fifteenth-century Europe knew Japan.

Discussion about the origin and interpretation of such islands ranges between two poles. On the one hand, there are those who consider all such islands to have been mere cartographical whimsy, designed simply to fill otherwise empty spaces on a map. On the other hand, some scholars insist that these islands represent otherwise unknown European discoveries in the Atlantic, a century or more before the voyages of Columbus and Cabot: St. Brendan's Isle might be Newfoundland, Brasil could be one of the Azores or even Bermuda, while Antilia might be Cuba or another Caribbean Island. The truth probably lies somewhere between these extremes. It seems unlikely that these islands are records of fourteenth or fifteenth-century transatlantic discovery, but they are probably more than mere figments of the late mediaeval European imagination. They may, in fact, be a vague remnant of European knowledge about the western discoveries of the Irish and the Norse.

The Portuguese Search

The search for remote Atlantic islands was led by the Portuguese who, under Prince Henry the Navigator, were the supreme explorers of the fifteenth century. Their search was stimulated by repeated successes at increasingly great distances from the Old World. The Canary Islands, 100 kilometres off the west coast of Africa, had been known since Roman times. They were inhabited by a Berber-like people known as the Guanches and were revisited by the Portuguese during the fourteenth century. The first previously unknown island to be discovered was Madeira, lying 500 kilometres further into the Atlantic. It was discovered shortly

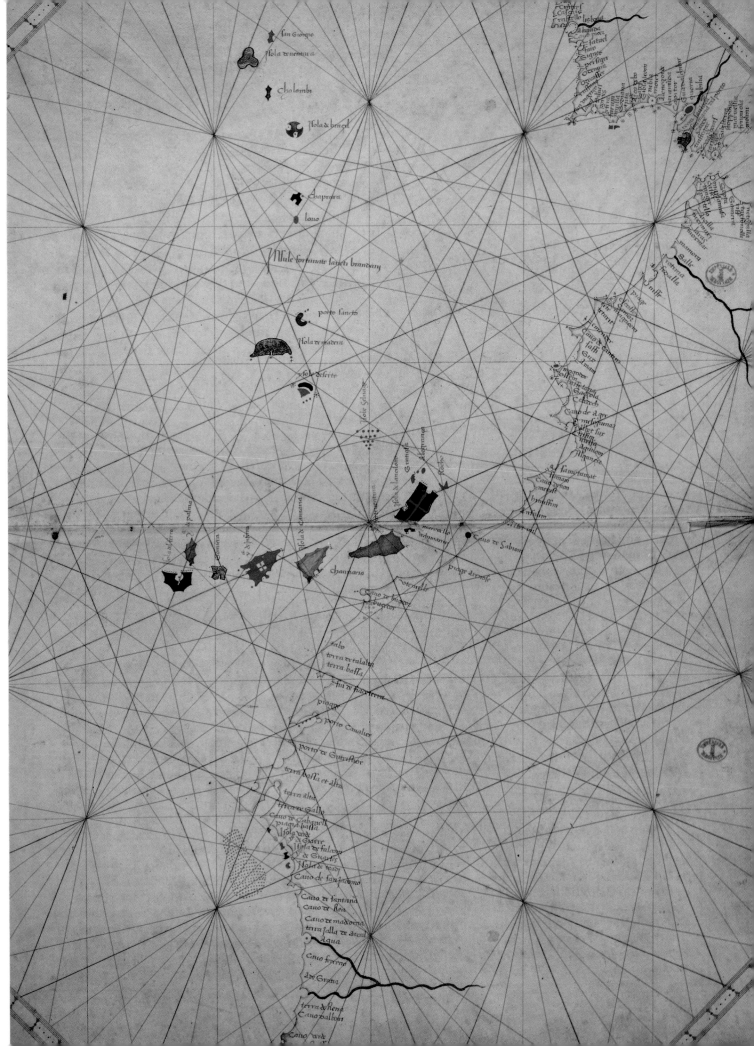

san Giorgio

ysola truentura

cholombi

ysola de brazil

chaprara

louo

Mule fortunate sancti brandany

porto sancto

ysola de madeira

ysole delerte

ysole Salueie

Longa

Roqua

ysola de lancelotus

Gentilis

maruxillo
echinsario

Cauo de Sabion

piage dronse

stranfer

Cauo de bugep
bucfor

Tabo
terra de talala
terra baffa

fin de ftacaferra

piage

porto caualier

porto de Guteafior

terra baffa et alta

terra alta

terra de Gallo
Cauo de Cabanel
piague baffa
ysola verde
d'Giarre
ysola de falcoa
de Guardie
ysola de raioy
Cauo de sanfacemo

Cauo de santana
Cauo de Rea
Cauo de madoena
terra falla de arena
aqua
Cauo ftreno
de Grena

terra de Rena
Cauo dalton

CHAPTER 6

THE NEWE FOUND ISLANDE

In 1497, John Cabot sailed from England, and reported the discovery of an island in the far northwestern Atlantic. A letter recently discovered in a Spanish archive now suggests that this "New Found Land" may have been discovered by Bristol fishermen before the voyages of either Cabot or Columbus.

To find their latitude, fifteenth-century navigators used the quadrant.
A simplified form of an astronomical instrument, the quadrant was a quarter-circle
of thin metal with an attached plumb-line,
and could be easily made by hand. (Height: 8.7 cm)

The 1490s are usually seen as the period when the major and lasting discoveries of the New World occurred. In 1492 Columbus sailed westward from Spain and found the islands of the Caribbean. Five years later, John Cabot made a voyage westward from England and discovered another island in the depths of the North Atlantic. The first of these voyages can be seen as leading to the birth of the Spanish civilization of Central and South America, the second, to the birth of the English civilization of North America.

The voyages of both Columbus and Cabot rank as major historical events, yet the amount which we know about the two Italian explorers is remarkably different: Columbus lived for a considerable time after his discoveries, long enough to describe his voyages in detail, gather honour and fame, and attain the Spanish title "Admiral of the Ocean Sea." Cabot disappeared the year after his successful voyage, leaving no written description of his work, no portrait, not even a signature on any document that historians have found. To make matters worse, his son Sebastian outlived his father by well over half a century, and claimed his father's discoveries as his own. Until the nineteenth century, Sebastian Cabot was treated by most historians as the English discoverer of North America. But historical fashions change, and by the first half of the present century the honour had been restored to the father, John.

Then in 1955 an historian working in the archives of Simancas, in Spain, discovered a document which seems to confirm John Cabot as the master of the first official English voyage to the New World, but places his voyage in the context of several earlier and unofficial voyages from the western English port of Bristol. Cabot was the explorer who officially claimed an English stake in the New World; but was he the first English voyager to that country which immediately became known as the New Found Land?

The John Day Letter

The document found in the Simancas archive, which was published in 1956, was an undated letter written in Spanish by an Englishman named John Day, addressed to "El Almirante Major." Christopher Columbus was the only Spanish official of the time who was referred to by this title, and the letter was almost certainly addressed to him. John Day is relatively well known from other records of the day as a Bristol merchant who had extensive trading interests in Spain. The purpose of his letter was to report that an unnamed explorer, sailing from England, had discovered an island in the western Atlantic. For this service, the King had granted the explorer an annual pension of 20 pounds, and had outfitted another expedition to take place in the following year. This information confirms that the explorer was John Cabot (who from other sources we know was granted such a pension by Henry VII), and dates the letter to the months between the return of Cabot's 1497 voyage and the departure of his ill-fated voyage of 1498.

To this point, the letter merely confirmed what had been pieced together from other records concerning John Cabot's place in English exploration. The John Day letter, however, went on to supply further information on English voyages to the west. A translation of the most interesting portion of the letter reads as follows:

It is considered certain that the cape of the said land [that is, the land found by Cabot in 1497] *was found and discovered in times past by the men of Bristol who found Brasil as your Lordship knows. It was called the Isle of Brasil and it is assumed and believed to be the mainland that the Bristol men found.*

The interpretation of this paragraph has been debated for the past 30 years. The main discussion has dealt with the meaning of the Spanish phrase "*en otros tiempos*" ("in other times" or "in times past"). Does this phrase refer to the year before Cabot's voyage, a decade earlier (which would place it before Columbus' "discovery" of the New World), or does it refer to a legendary event lost in the mists of antiquity, and therefore not to be regarded as serious history? The respected English historian David Quinn has made a close study of the problem, and has concluded that the John Day letter confirms other evidence suggesting the possibility of English discoveries in the western Atlantic at least a decade before Columbus' first voyage.

The evidence in support of John Day's statement comes from various local records and histories, generally centred around the port of Bristol. The earliest is from the year 1480, and

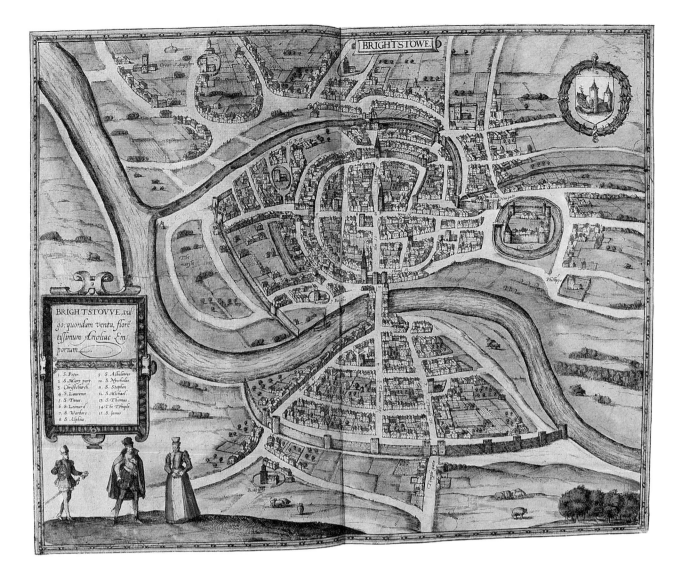

states that a ship left Bristol for the island of Brasil to the west of Ireland, but was storm-tossed and returned without having found the island. The following year, several records refer to two Bristol ships, the *George* and *Trinity*, which sailed to "serch & fynde a certain Isle called the Isle of Brasile." One of these ships, the *George*, carried 40 bushels of salt, an indication that fishing as well as exploration was an object of the voyage. The ships returned, but there is no mention of what they found or did not find. The partners who supported the 1481 voyage of the *George* and *Trinity* had a license to make further voyages during the following two years, but no record of these voyages has been found.

In 1498, a Spanish official in London, reporting to the King of Spain on Cabot's voyage of the previous year, stated that, "For the past seven years the people of Bristol have equipped two, three or four caravels to go in search of the Island of Brasil and the Seven Cities according to the fancy of this Genoese" (the Genoese re-

Bristol in 1572. A register from 1498 shows that John Cabot had a house not far from the port. From its position on the Atlantic coast, Bristol dominated fifteenth-century English commerce with Iceland to the north and Portugal to the south.

ferred to being John Cabot). In a document which dates to 1527 Robert Thorne, son of a Bristol merchant of the same name, claimed that his father and another merchant named Hugh Elyot were the discoverers of "the New Found Landes." Quinn concludes that the English had likely discovered something in the western Atlantic several years before the voyage of Cabot, and probably before the voyage of Columbus in 1492.

Bristol Fishermen and Merchants

If the theory of a pre-Cabotean discovery is correct, what sort of find are the men of Bristol likely to have made? Why would their discovery not have been hailed, as was that of Columbus, as a major event in European exploration? Why would John Cabot, an immigrant navigator from Italy, have later been rewarded for discovering new land in the west? The most likely explanation would seem to be one that takes into account the motives which would have propelled sailors from the port of Bristol into the western Atlantic during the final decades of the fifteenth century.

English sailors certainly had the ships, the navigational abilities and the experience to make extensive ocean voyages at this time. The extent of the voyages made by English fishermen is suggested in a note compiled about 1478 by the English chronicler William Worcestre, who records that around the beginning of the fifteenth century, Iceland had been accidentally discovered by "Robert Bacon, a seaman among the fishers of Cromer town, of English birth." Throughout most of the century, Bristol had been one of the leading English ports engaged in trading and fishing in Icelandic waters. Not only had Iceland provided a market for English goods, but it was also the major source of the stockfish (dried cod) which was such a valuable commodity to English merchants. The Icelandic trade and fishery was not pursued without problems, including sporadic states of war between England and Denmark, which ruled Iceland at the time. Denmark was naturally

Christopher Columbus' Nina is chosen to illustrate the ships used by late fifteenth-century explorers, since we know more about her than about any other ship of the period.
The Santa Clara, nicknamed Nina, was less than 20 m long and had a cargo capacity of only about 50 tonnes. She was a caravel with lateen rig, which Columbus re-rigged with square sails during a stop at the Canary Islands.

within the sphere of influence of the northern German Hanseatic League, and Hanseatic ships had royal permission to trade with Iceland. Denmark repeatedly complained to England about English ships in Icelandic waters. Such ships were reported to be engaged in unlicensed fishing, trading, and even coastal raiding and kidnapping of Icelanders. In 1478, Denmark installed a German, Diddrik Pining, as governor of Iceland, and for the next twelve years Pining successfully drove most English shipping from Icelandic coasts.

It is perhaps no coincidence that the first records of Bristol ships searching for, or visiting, an island in the western Atlantic occurred only two years after Pining began his campaign to put an end to English fishing and trading in Iceland. The ships engaged in the Atlantic search were almost certainly the same ones that had previously engaged in Icelandic ventures, and it can probably be assumed that they

John Cabot's Route

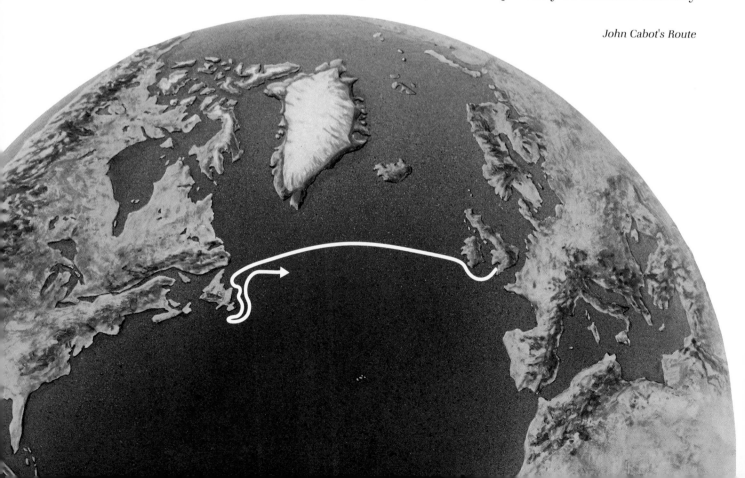

raised tables of twigs an
which the fish were cur
which can still be seen i
coast villages.

Sun-cured codfish h
weight and texture of a li
will last indefinitely if kep
is easily reconstituted by
water. It became Canada
major export to the worl
food throughout western
and the Caribbean, and t

The history ɛ
erally linkeᵈ
national syⁿ
basis of the fur trɑ
northern North Aᵣ
European econoⁿ
probably deserves
recognition, as the
first drew Europeɑ
eastern shores of tʰ
as the economic bɑ
successful Europeɑ
the Atlantic coast.

The cod is a grɛ
northern waters thɑ
shallow seas overlyⁱ
shelves. Long befoᵣ
land was discovereᵈ
become a staple of ɑ
European diet whicʰ
abstinence from mᵉ
more days of the wᵉ
white flesh, fine tastᵉ
and excellent storagᵉ
codfish a prominent
pean subsistence. Tʰ

of northern Europe sᵉ
stantly for new and pᵣ
ing grounds, and by tʰ
fifteenth century mosᵗ
being taken from Icelɑ

John Cabot's 1497
the codfish were so thⁱ
waters off his "Newe Fᵉ
that they could be takᵉ
let down from the sidᵉ
was met with great enᵗ
fishermen of England ɑ
European countries. Aᵣ
low fishing banks off N

were seeking the same opportunities: markets for English goods, but more importantly an alternate supply of codfish to replace what they could no longer obtain in Iceland.

David Quinn conjectures that if Bristol ships did discover land in the northwestern Atlantic, it may have been important to them only as a marker indicating the location of a new and extremely rich fishing ground off the coasts of Newfoundland. The fishermen of Bristol may not have seen any riches, or indeed any use, in an island such as Newfoundland; it certainly would have yielded no precious metals, spices or other trade, and the fishermen may have gone ashore only in order to obtain water. They would have seen no advantage to proclaiming their discovery, particularly if it advertised the location of new fishing grounds. In such a situation, and in the context of the recent discoveries of Columbus, a navigator like John Cabot who had lived in Spain and who saw other potentialities in the rumours of a newly discovered island — as a station on the road to China rather than the marker of a fishing ground — may have easily obtained royal approval for an official English voyage of discovery in the west.

Who Was John Cabot?

Although most twentieth-century Canadian schoolchildren are taught that Canada was discovered by John Cabot, we know remarkably little about the man or about his voyages of discovery. He was probably born Giovanni Caboto, but his place of birth is not certain. Some records from the time of his voyages refer to him as a native of Genoa, but no Genoese archive has produced a trace of his existence. He may have been born in Genoa (probably about the same time as that other famous Genoese explorer, Christopher Columbus), but his family seems to have moved to Venice while he was a boy, and he became a citizen of that city in 1476. He seems to have established himself as a merchant, involved in the Venetian trade with Arab countries around the eastern Mediterranean. He is said to have made a trip to Mecca, probably disguised as an Islamic pilgrim in order to penetrate that holy city.

In 1484 we have a record that he was married with two sons, but he then disappears from historical records for over a decade, reappearing in England around 1495. It seems likely, however, that in the intervening period he appears in Spanish records as Juan Caboto Montecalunya, a navigator who began about 1490 to approach Spanish and Portuguese officials with a scheme to sail westward across the Atlantic in order to reach the Orient. At the time that Columbus was granted permission to undertake such a voyage, Juan Caboto was acting as a consultant on a harbour project in Valencia, where he must have been in a good position to learn firsthand the results of Columbus' successful expedition.

Having been forestalled in his plans to discover a route to the Orient by sailing westward from Spain, Cabot may have decided that better opportunities lay in England. Not only must the English king be feeling somewhat behind his southern rivals in nautical discoveries, but a glance at a globe (such as the one Cabot made in 1497 to show the King) would indicate that England's northern latitude provided a potentially short route to the Orient. If Columbus could discover the outliers of India by sailing the long route westward from Spain, Cabot could surely find the outliers of Cathay by sailing across the narrow longitudes west of Ireland. Accordingly, Cabot and his family arrived in England at some time around 1495, settled in Bristol, and began petitioning the King for a licence to undertake, at his own expense, an expedition to place the British flag on an Oriental land.

Did Cabot have other reasons for selecting Bristol as a base for a northern voyage? Had he heard the rumours of earlier Bristol expeditions in search of the Isle of Brasil? Or had he heard stories originating in Iceland regarding land in the western Atlantic? Some scholars have suggested that Cabot, like his fellow-explorer Columbus, made a journey to Iceland. Cabot has even been identified, on the basis of no sound evidence, with "The Guest at Ingjoldsholl"; according to an Icelandic folk-tale, the guest was a "Latin man" who arrived at Snaefellsnes about this time in a ship from Bristol, and who lived there for some time while inquiring about exploration in the western Atlantic

If Cabot did travel to Iceland, he undoubtedly could have heard accounts of the Greenland colony to the west, which must have still been alive in Icelandic memory, and possibly of Norse voyages to Markland and Vinland. Yet Cabot could equally well have heard such sto-

*Attributed to Juan de la Cosa,
owner of the Santa Maria and
companion of Columbus, this map
drawn in 1500 shows the oldest
known representation of the West
Indies. It also shows, in its northern
section, the only trace of John
Cabot's voyage known from
a contemporaneous map. Along
a northern section of coast are five
English flags, and the inscription
mar descubierta por inglese
(Sea discovered by an Englishman),
which must represent the land
discovered by the Venetian
navigator sailing in the service of
Henry VII (see detail).*

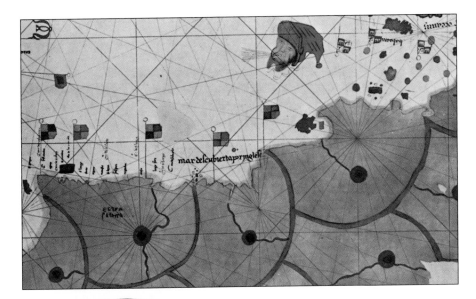

ries without leaving Bristol, the centre for English fishing and trading with Iceland. According to an alien census roll of 1484, 48 Icelanders were resident in Bristol at that time. Most were working as servants, and some had perhaps been captured in English raids on Icelandic settlements, but at least one (a William Yslond) had become a naturalized citizen and a Bristol merchant by 1492. Tales of land to the west, originating either from Icelandic contacts or from fishermen talking of the Isle of Brasil, may have been among the considerations which attracted John Cabot to the city of Bristol. If he had not heard such tales before he came to Bristol, he must certainly have been told them while residing in that city and discussing his plans for a voyage of discovery. By the time he sailed, Cabot must have been well aware of local rumours about what he could expect to find in the western Atlantic.

The Cabot Voyages

Cabot received a royal warrant to explore westward from England in 1496, and according to the John Day letter he did undertake a voyage that year, but was turned back by a discouraged and mutinous crew. Undaunted, he fitted out a small ship named the *Mathew* the following year and sailed westward once again. Despite the fact that the 1497 expedition resulted in the discovery of North America, we know surprisingly little about the details of the voyage. English records relating to the discovery are practically nonexistent. Until 1955 the main sources of information were two reports written by Italian diplomats in England. The discovery of the John Day letter, however, added a significant amount of new information about the 1497 voyage.

Our knowledge of Cabot's 1497 voyage is easily summarized. The *Mathew* left Bristol in late May and probably set course for southern Ireland, finally departing from somewhere in the southwest of that country. They sailed for 35 days before easterly and northeasterly winds, encountered one storm, and made landfall early in the morning of St. John's Day, June 24. The party went ashore in a forested area close to their landfall, and set up a cross bearing the papal arms and the arms of the King of England. They found a path leading into the woods, a spot where a fire had been made, snares for animals and a red-painted stick which might have been a netting needle. These signs of

human habitation seem to have caused them some anxiety, and they did not explore farther inland than a cross-bow shot. They took on fresh water, rowed back to the ship and did not go ashore again for the remainder of the voyage.

They explored the coast for about a month, seeing fine forests, what they thought might have been cultivated fields, but no people save for two creatures seen in the distance which might have been humans or animals. They also found that the coastal waters teemed with codfish, in such dense concentrations that they could be caught in weighted baskets let down over the side of the ship. Cabot then returned to his original landfall, and departed for a remarkable 15-day return trip to Europe. During this leg of the voyage the crew convinced him that he was steering too far north, so he altered course to the south but made a landfall in Brittany. He had to work his way northward to Bristol, where he arrived on August 6. Cabot left immediately for London to report his discovery, and on August 10 King Henry VII awarded the sum of 10 pounds "to hym that founde the new Isle."

This reward was supplemented some months later by an annual pension of 20 pounds, and a licence to make another voyage the following year in order to begin exploitation of the new discovery. In May 1498, Cabot set out across the Atlantic at the head of a convoy of five ships. One was damaged in a storm and returned to Ireland, and the other four disappeared. Thus John Cabot vanishes from historical records within a year of his great discovery; his pension was cancelled the following year. In the words of the contemporary historian Polydore Virgil, "He is believed to have found the new lands only at the bottom of the ocean."

What Did Cabot Discover?

Before the John Day letter came to light, there was no precise information on the location of Cabot's "newe found islande." As in the case of the Norse in North America, local or regional interests produced differing interpretations of the vague evidence available, and developed arguments to support Cabot's having landed anywhere from Labrador to New England. Newfoundlanders have always been convinced that their island was the obvious candidate. Before the 1949 confederation between Canada and Newfoundland, Canadians found this hard to accept and most Canadian historians chose Cape Breton as the likely landfall. This alternative also had the advantage of making Cabot the discoverer of mainland North America, since prior to 1498 Columbus had discovered and visited only Caribbean islands. Some American scholars, not surprisingly, have suggested that Cabot's landing may have occurred on the coast of Maine.

John Day's letter to Christopher Columbus seems to have finally settled the argument. According to the letter, Cabot thought he had dis-

instruments of the time, and the fact that Cabot must have measured his most southerly latitude from shipboard rather than from land, it seems almost certain that the region of the New World which Cabot discovered and explored was the eastern coast of Newfoundland. The statement that "the cape closest to Ireland is 1800 millas west of Dursey Head" fits this interpretation, if the "milla" is anything like a modern mile, and considering that fifteenth-century navigators based their calculations of longitude on little more than guesswork; Cape Bauld is approximately 1600 nautical miles (or 1800 standard miles) west of Dursey Head. The interpretation of Newfoundland as part main-

Latitude is calculated by measuring the height of the noon sun above the horizon. The cross-staff or Jacob's staff replaced the quadrant as the favoured instrument of mariners. The cross-staff was a wooden rod with a peep-hole at one end, and a sliding cross-piece. The navigator placed his eye against one end of the staff, and slid the cross-piece until he saw the lower tip at the horizon and the upper tip at the sun or North Star. The altitude of the celestial body could then be read from a scale marked on the main staff.

covered the easternmost cape of mainland Asia, as well as one or more islands adjacent to it. Day reports that "the cape closest to Ireland is 1,800 millas west of Dursey Head, which is in Ireland, and the lowest part of the Isle of Seven Cities is west of the River of Bordeaux." Dursey Head is in southwestern Ireland, at a latitude of 51° 33' N; the River of Bordeaux must be the Gironde, the mouth of which lies at a latitude of 45° 40' N. Cape Bauld, the northern tip of the island of Newfoundland, lies in latitude 51° 39' N, only six nautical miles (10 kilometres) farther north than Dursey Head in Ireland. Cape Race, at the southeastern corner of Newfoundland, lies at 46° 40' N, roughly 60 miles (100 kilometres) north of the latitude of the Gironde. Considering the imprecision of navigational

land and part island is not surprising, considering the several deep bays which indent the eastern coast; maps a century or more later showed Newfoundland as a cluster of islands.

Not all historians agree that the description in the John Day letter indicates that Newfoundland was the only area discovered by Cabot. David Quinn, for example, holds with Cape Breton (at 45° 57' N, only 17 nautical miles north of the latitude of the Gironde) as Cabot's landfall, followed by a month-long journey eastward and northward, and a departure from Newfoundland in the vicinity of Cape Bauld. A more persuasive argument, however, is put forward by the American historian Samuel Eliot Morison, whose study of documents is augmented by a deep knowledge of sailing and sailing ships, and by marine and aerial surveys of most of the east coast of North America. Morison argues that Cabot probably practiced the "latitude sailing" commonly used at the time; he departed from Ireland somewhere in the vicinity of Dursey Head, and sailed westward along a line of latitude by keeping the sun and the pole star at a constant elevation. This would have brought him to the northern tip of Newfoundland, and Morison guesses that Cabot went ashore and raised his cross in what is now Griquet harbour. He considers that a month of exploration would be appropriate for a journey down the eastern coast of Newfoundland, and for the return to the original landfall which is suggested in the John Day letter. He further argues, rather convincingly, that it would have been very difficult for Cabot to have reached Cape Breton without running into Newfoundland, or at least seeing it to the north while crossing the extensive Grand Banks.

If Morison's interpretation is correct, and it does seem to be the one that best fits the information contained in the John Day letter, it suggests that Cabot's original landfall was only a few kilometers from the Norse settlement at L'Anse aux Meadows. This could have been, of course, the result of pure coincidence brought about through Cabot's technique of "latitude sailing" from a departure point in southern Ireland. On the other hand, Cabot may have been navigating purposefully towards the northern end of the Strait of Belle Isle, a location which figures largely in the very early European history of Canada. Knowledge of the location may

have come from any of three sources: Icelandic records or memories of the location of Vinland; the accounts of Bristol fishermen who had visited the locality a few years before Cabot, and whose knowledge again may have been originally based on Icelandic sources; or European geographical knowledge of the kind that may have been incorporated in the "Vinland Map" half a century earlier.

Was John Cabot Searching for China, or for Newfoundland?

We are left with the suspicion that John Cabot may have known where he was going when he sailed westward from Bristol. His discovery of North America may not have been the lucky result of an attempt to reach Cathay, based on a purely theoretical concept of world geography. He may have been travelling to a known location, which he incorrectly interpreted as an outlier of Asia. This interpretation implies a continuity of European knowledge about eastern Canada, from Norse times to the Renaissance. We know that the Greenlandic Norse were visiting eastern Canada at least as recently as 1347. If the historian David Quinn is correct, Bristol fishermen may have been making use of the area as early as 1480, and perhaps before the final demise of the Greenlandic Norse settlements. The remarkable voyage of John Cabot may, therefore, not have been a voyage of discovery, but merely another event in a continuous series of European visits to the region over the previous 500 years.

CHAPTER 7

THE LABRADOR

Did the Portuguese discover Canada? We know that by A.D. 1500, Portuguese navigators had rediscovered Greenland, and were exploring and raiding the eastern coasts of Canada. Within twenty years they had established a settlement in Nova Scotia, and Canada appeared destined to become a Portuguese colony.

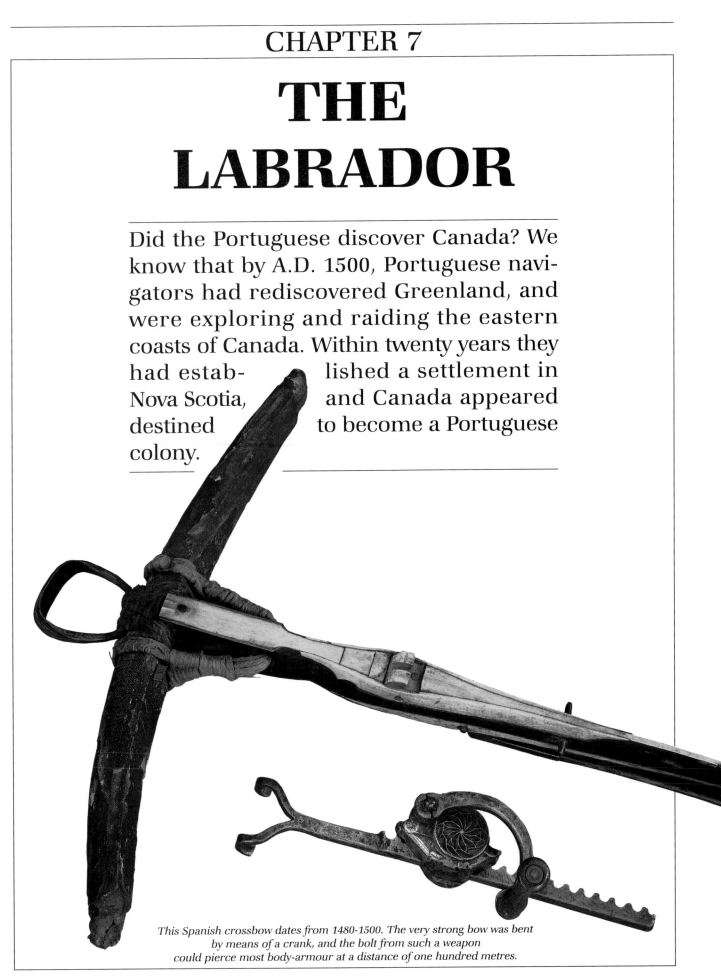

This Spanish crossbow dates from 1480-1500. The very strong bow was bent by means of a crank, and the bolt from such a weapon could pierce most body-armour at a distance of one hundred metres.

Several European nations were involved in the fifteenth-century search for Atlantic islands. In the previous chapter, we have seen that from about 1480 onwards, the merchants and navigators of Bristol sent several expeditions into the western Atlantic, mostly in search of the "Isle of Brasil." This search culminated in Cabot's discovery of Newfoundland in 1497, and it has been suggested that this event may have merely followed earlier English discoveries in the area. There is also a possibility that the Portuguese had made pre-Cabotian and even pre-Columbian discoveries in the northwestern Atlantic.

The Portuguese led the early European search for Atlantic islands. By the 1450s they had discovered and settled the Canaries, Madeira, the Cape Verdes and the Azores. The latter islands lay in mid-Atlantic, almost halfway between Portugal and Newfoundland, and were to provide the base for early sixteenth-century Portuguese exploration farther to the west and north.

Built on the Restelo, *the shore from which so many voyages of exploration departed, the Bélem tower in Lisbon dates from the early years of the sixteenth century. Its decorative motifs evoke scenes from Portuguese exploration.*

Land West of The Azores?

The Portuguese discovery and settlement of the Azores provided these expert explorers with a far western base from which to launch further expeditions. It also gave them clear indications that there was land worth searching for to the west. The Azores are bathed by a northwesterly ocean current, an offshoot of the Gulf Stream which carries flotsam picked up from the eastern shores of North America. Writing of the evidence Columbus had gathered prior to his 1492 voyage of discovery, the sixteenth century author Bartolomé de las Casas states that:

It was made known to Columbus by some inhabitants of the Azores that when the wind blew strong from the west and north-west the sea brought certain pine-trunks and deposited them on the coasts of those islands... Others told him that in the island of Flores, which is one of the Azores, the sea had brought up the bodies of two dead men who seemed very broad in the face and of an appearance different from that of Christians... [He was also told of] *hollowed trunks or canoes with a moveable covering ...* [which had been accidentally blown offshore and] *... since they never sink, came to land in time at the Azores.*

Such indications of land to the west or northwest, and land inhabited by people who used strange boats and had "an appearance different from that of Christians," must have encouraged early Azorean settlers to make further explorations in this quadrant. The first occurred in 1452, and resulted in the discovery of Corvo and Flores, the two westernmost Azorean islands. The discoverers, Pedro de Velasco and Diogo de Tieve, are said to have sailed to the north as well, where they eventually landed in Ireland. During this voyage they were caught in a heavy westerly storm, but since the seas remained calm despite the west wind, they suspected they were sailing in the lee of a land they did not see. According to Las Casas, Columbus was told a similar story by "a decrepit old sailor" who, on a voyage to Ireland, sighted a land believed to be Tartary, which the ship could not approach because of terrible winds. Las Casas states that he "believes truly (that this land) was that which we now call Bacallaos," the sixteenth century Portuguese name for Newfoundland.

This soldier tightens the string on his crossbow. Having placed his foot in the stirrup as a brace, he winds the crank until the cord reaches a stop, which will be released by the trigger when the weapon is fired. He wears a garment made of rivetted metal plates over a leather vest.

Portuguese court records from the second half of the fifteenth century contain several licences, patents and grants to islands not yet discovered, issued to a variety of mainland and Azorean navigators. There is no evidence that any of these explorers actually claimed discov-

eries to the west of the Azores, yet there are indications in the cartography of the period hinting that something may have been found far northwest of the Azores.

The Milan Chart and the Paris Map

The first such hint appears on a Spanish chart of the Atlantic Ocean, apparently drawn about 1480, now in a library in Milan and consequently known as the Milan Chart. The British Isles and Iceland are drawn in some detail; the latter is labelled *Fixlanda* and contains a number of local placenames. The map also portrays a few of the familiar mythical islands, including a small circular Isle of Brasil to the west of Ireland. South of it lies the mythical island of *Mayda*, usually associated with the Azores. Far to the northwest is a larger *Illa de Brazil* nestled into the southern bay of a large rectangular island labelled *Illa Verde*. This is a new configuration not known on earlier maps, and it shows the conjunction of four previously disparate phenomena to form an interesting and perhaps significant pattern:

(1) The narrow rectangular form of *Illa Verde* appears to be clearly derived from that of "Antilia" or "The Isle of Seven Cities" as it is shown on other fifteenth-century maps, and may represent this island in a new location and under a new name.

(2) This island is closely associated with the Isle of Brasil, which had hitherto been seen as a totally separate island with a separate history and location.

(3) Both islands are shown at roughly the latitude of Ireland, southwest of Iceland and northwest of the Azores, and forming a roughly equilateral triangle with Ireland and Iceland.

(4) The name *Illa Verde* (Green Island) may be related to Greenland, a name and a place which hovered on the margins of fifteenth-century European knowledge of the northern Atlantic.

What does this conjunction suggest about the knowledge available to the unknown cartographer who drew the Milan Chart? It might suggest that about A.D. 1480, he had heard of a discovery in the ocean, far to the west of Ireland and northwest of the Azores. Whatever he had heard, the news may have been sufficiently convincing to suggest that it accounted for both Antilia and Brasil, the foremost mythical islands

Divine Right

When John Cabot sailed from Bristol in 1497, he carried a document from King Henry VII granting "to our well-beloved John Cabot" the authority to discover and investigate islands or countries "of heathens or infidels, in whatsoever part of the world placed, which were before this time unknown to all Christians." Cabot and his sons were granted the right to "conquer, occupy and possess" any such countries or towns which they discovered, and to obtain title and dominion to these countries and towns on behalf of the King of England. Most other explorers of the period carried similar charters or letters patent, giving them the rights to claim ownership of newly-discovered territories in the names of their monarchs.

On what authority did the kings of European nations base their rights to discover, conquer and obtain title to other regions of the earth? As we can see from the charter to John Cabot, this authority was obviously based on a religious theory of ownership and title to land, which had developed through the European Middle Ages and was refined during the Crusades. According to this doctrine, the world was the property of the Christian God, who granted stewardship of worldly affairs to the Pope of the Christian church; European rulers, in turn, derived their authority from the Pope, in return for fealty and temporal support. Heathens and infidels had no place in this scheme of world ownership, and their lands were forfeit to the first Christians who could take them by force, guile

In 1271 Venetian merchants of the Polo family made their second overland venture to China, where they were received by Kublai Khan. This miniature from the Book of Marvels *shows the travellers presenting the Mongol emperor with a letter from Pope Gregory X.*

or simple bluff. Applications of this theory of world ownership were not universally accepted. In 1245, Pope Innocent IV sent a delegation to the Mongol capitol of Karakorum, berating the Khan of the Mongols for overrunning eastern Europe four years previously, and advising him to become baptised. The Mongol ruler Kuyuk, nephew of Chingis Khan, replied that according to Mongol beliefs the world was divided into East and West, with the dividing line in what is now Poland. They acknowledged the Pope's supremacy in the West, but pointed out that his authority ended at the Vistula River, east of which lay the Eastern lands owned by the Mongols.

Ironically, it was the Mongol conquest from the Vistula to the Pacific that opened the way to trade between Europe and the Orient and eventually led to European attempts to obtain Asiatic goods by sea routes around Africa or westward across

the Atlantic. This, in turn, led to another division of the world into East and West, based on the papal proclamations of 1493. These decisions and the subsequent treaty of Tordesillas drew a mid-Atlantic demarcation line between the territories which could be acquired by Portugal in the east, and by Spain in the west.

The rate of discovery and the profits of exploitation which developed during the early sixteenth century, as well as the rise of protestant schism within the Church, soon diminished papal authority to assign zones of ownership. During the early sixteenth century the papacy was involved in answering a different question: whether the newly discovered peoples of the New World were to be considered as humans. In 1537 the Pope issued two proclamations stating that, "Man is of such condition and nature that he can receive the faith of Christ, and whoever has the nature of man is fitted to receive the same faith." The New World peoples were proclaimed to be as human as European Christians, could be allowed baptism and converted to Christianity, and could not be enslaved. The papacy was unclear, however, as to whether the heathen nations of the New World had the right to hold land and to prevent Christian occupation of their countries.

These ancient decisions, made on the basis of a politico-religious theory which has long been obsolete, are still relevant today. The inherent contradictions in Europe's attitudes to the First Peoples of the Americas — as people who were equal to Europeans before God, but who had less than equal rights to hold land and to govern their own societies — are the basis for most of the military and legal confrontations that still plague relations between the aboriginal peoples and newcomers to the New World.

of the Atlantic. The northwestern Atlantic position of this discovery may have suggested identifying at least one portion of the new land with Greenland, which was known from Icelandic and other northern European accounts to exist in the far northwest. Finally, the latitude and position relative to Iceland and the Azores suggest that the new discovery may have been located somewhere in the region of Labrador, Newfoundland or Nova Scotia. Did the supposed discovery occur during Azorean voyages such as those recorded by Las Casas as part of the knowledge assembled by Columbus? Did this discovery, or the existence of charts such as this, encourage Bristol fishermen to begin making western voyages about 1480, in search of an Isle of Brasil which was pictured as part of a larger Greenland configuration in the far west?

There are some similarities between the 1480 Milan Chart and another map drawn about a decade later, perhaps in Portugal. The latter is usually referred to as the Paris Map, and some attribute it to Christopher Columbus. It shows a well-delineated Iceland, a clear representation of the Azores, and a small Isle of Brasil southwest of Ireland. Far to the west of Ireland, in about the position of *Illa Verde* on the Milan Chart, is a tight cluster of three islands; these are labelled the "Island of the Seven Cities, now settled by the Portuguese." As mentioned in an earlier chapter, "Seven Cities" was a Portuguese synonym for the mythical island of Antilia, but this location is far northwest of the position that the island had been given on earlier maps. Here, too, for the first time the island is not drawn as a conventional rectangle with a few unconvincing bays or fabricated place-names. The coasts of the three islands are drawn realistically, and almost remind us of sixteenth-century maps of Newfoundland, which was usually represented as a cluster of islands. As on the Milan Chart, the new configuration forms almost an equilateral triangle with Iceland and Ireland, almost a square if the Azores are placed at the fourth corner. Again, this location hints at knowledge of a discovery made in the vicinity of Atlantic Canada, perhaps a Portuguese discovery, and perhaps even the establishment of a Portuguese settlement prior to the voyage of Christopher Columbus. Portuguese historians have unconvincingly linked this discovery with the name Joao Vaz Corte-Real, who is said to have made a voyage of discovery at some time around the

1470s. Unfortunately, this voyage is first mentioned over a century later in a document that is not considered trustworthy. Most non-Portuguese scholars have discounted the voyage of Joao Vaz Corte-Real, and give him credit only for raising sons who did make voyages of discovery a generation later.

The Treaty of Tordesillas

Columbus' 1492 discovery of the West Indies led to intense diplomatic activity designed to establish what would now be known as "national spheres of influence" in the areas of the world which various European nations were exploring. Spain and Portugal were the leading nations in exploration of the tropical and subtropical oceans. Columbus' voyage had given Spain its first and most important stake in western exploration; Portugal's primary efforts had been in the east, where for decades their navigators had gradually been pushing their way around the coasts of Africa. The Vatican soon became involved in defining the spheres of influence of the rival nations, and two papal bulls in 1493 recognized Portuguese interest in the east and Spanish in the west. This division was formalized in the Treaty of Tordesillas, signed in 1494, which placed the line of division between Spanish and Portuguese interest at a point 370 leagues (about 1,800 kilometres) west of the Cape Verde Islands.

These islands lie about 25° west of the African coast. The line of demarcation thus lay far to the west of Europe and Africa, but substantially to the east of Columbus' Caribbean discoveries. Considering how hard it was to make accurate measurements of longitude at that time, it is clear that no one knew exactly where the Spanish-Portuguese boundary lay. The treaty, however, did encourage the Portuguese to look further north and south for lands lying east of the line. They explored and settled the Brazilian portion of South America; and Brazil remains the only Portuguese-speaking nation of the New World. In the north, the only portions of the New World that could conceivably lie within the Portuguese sphere were Newfoundland, Labrador and Greenland. And indeed, these lands saw significant Portuguese exploration during the first quarter of the sixteenth century.

The Labrador

On October 28, 1499, King Manuel of Portugal signed a patent promising a certain Joao Fernandes the governorship of any islands

Routes of Portuguese Explorers

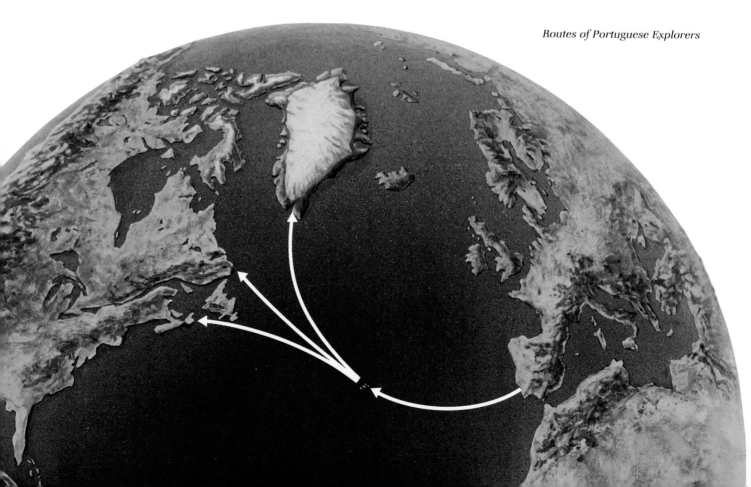

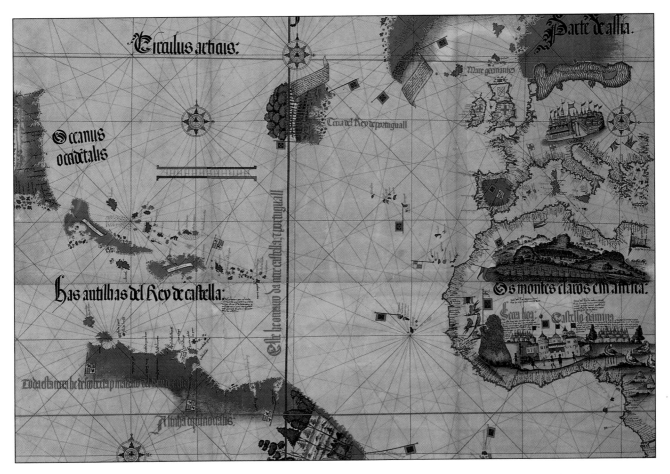

which he found in the west. Fernandes was a native of the island of Terceira in the Azores; he was referred to as a *lavrador*, an Azorean title meaning that he was a small landholder. He appears to have had some commercial connection with the English port of Bristol, and through his acquaintances there, was probably kept abreast of the results of the Cabot voyages. Through his Bristol connections he may also have picked up Icelandic stories of Greenland, for that was where he headed his ship in 1500.

The results of Fernandes' voyage are known only from inscriptions on early sixteenth-century maps. A Portuguese map drawn in 1502 for an Italian envoy named Alberto Cantino contains a reasonable depiction of southern Greenland. Beside this configuration, an inscription states that, "This land was discovered by order of the very excellent Prince Dom Manoel, King of Portugal, which it is believed is a point of Asia. Those who discovered it did not land, but they saw very rugged mountains, whence, according to the opinion of cosmographers, it is believed to be the peninsula of Asia." On other maps of the time, the Greenland configuration is labelled *Terra Laboratoris* or *Terra Laurador*. An inscription on a 1527 map states that the

In 1494, the Treaty of Tordesillas fixed a line of demarcation which divided the world into two zones of influence: Spanish in the west and Portuguese in the east. A map from 1502, of which this is a facsimile, shows the line clearly at what seems to be approximately 60° west longitude. In South America, Brazil is on the Portuguese side of the line, while in the north, Newfoundland is labelled Terra del Rey de Portuguall *(Land of the King of Portugal).*

Land of the Labrador "was discovered by the English of the town of Bristol. They gave it that name because he who gave them directions was a lavrador of the Azores."

This inscription seems to confirm that after his voyage to Greenland, Fernandes returned to Bristol rather than to the Azores, and formed an exploration consortium with certain merchants of that city. In 1501, Henry VII issued letters patent to a group of merchants from Bristol and the Azores, among them Joao Fernandes. This letter, and a second in 1502, granted exclusive licence to trade and exploit newly discovered lands in the west, but with the proviso "always that they in no wise occupy themselves with nor enter the lands...first discovered by the subjects of our very dear brother and cousin the King of Portugal."

Fagundes had apparently already made a voyage along the southern coast of Newfoundland, and perhaps through Cabot Strait into the Gulf of St. Lawrence, naming several islands which he had discovered. Scholars have identified these islands with various islands which exist today between Nova Scotia, Sable Island and eastern Newfoundland. The only convincing identification, however, is Fagundes' "*ilha de Pitiguoem*" with what are today known as the Penguin Islands, lying 20 kilometres off the southwestern coast of Newfoundland. The penguin of the sixteenth century was the now-extinct Great Auk, a bird vulnerable to human predation which could exist only on isolated offshore rocks that were rarely or never visited by canoe-borne aboriginal hunters. Since several of the named islands were west of Penguin Island, this identification places Fagundes in the general Cape Breton-southwestern Newfoundland region prior to his 1521 receipt of royal letters-patent. The map legend cited earlier may have truthfully named him the discoverer of Nova Scotia.

How Fagundes used his royal licence is a more obscure problem. One of the very few

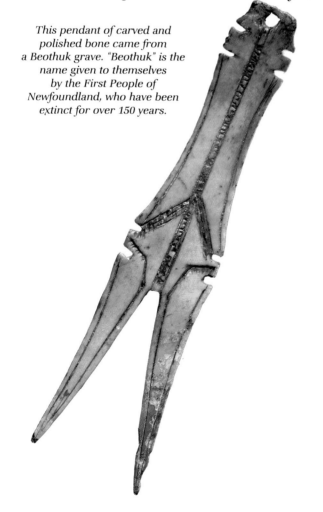

This pendant of carved and polished bone came from a Beothuk grave. "Beothuk" is the name given to themselves by the First People of Newfoundland, who have been extinct for over 150 years.

The Portuguese began the slave trade in Canada. In 1501 Gaspar Corte-Real's crew captured 57 men and women from Terra Verde, to be sold as slaves; the people were probably Beothuks from Newfoundland. Seven years later, the French captain Thomas Aubert followed the Portuguese example by abducting a group of Beothuks to Dieppe.

documents which mention him simply states that, "Joam Alvarez Fagundes discovered Terra Nova, or the country now called Cape Breton, which the king granted to him, and where he established cod fisheries which became a large source of profit to Portugal...." Another document, dating from the late sixteenth century, tells of a venture carried out between 1520 and 1525 by "certain gentlemen of Vianna"; since Fagundes was a native of Vianna, we may assume that he was associated with this enterprise. The story involves two shiploads of settlers who attempted to establish a colony in Newfoundland, almost certainly a shore-station to be used for drying salt-cod. Finding the area too cold, they settled on another coast to the west:

And as they had lost their ships, nothing further was heard from them, save from the Basques who continue to visit that coast in search of the many articles to be obtained there, who bring out word of them and state that they asked them to let us know how they were, and to take out priests; for the natives are submissive and the soil very fertile and good.... This is at Cape Breton, at the beginning of the coast that runs north, in a beautiful bay, where there are many people and goods of much value and many nuts, chestnuts, grapes and other fruits, whereby it is clear the soil is rich.... May the Lord in his mercy open a way by which to succour them.

The location of this colony, the first attempt by sixteenth-century Europeans to establish a land base in North America, is not known. The primary clue comes from the report quoted above, which suggests the eastern coast of Cape Breton Island as the most likely locality. Another support for this interpretation appears on several Portuguese maps drawn after 1550. Most of the place-names on these maps are in Portuguese or French, except for a set of five along the eastern coast of Cape Breton Island, which seem to be Micmac.

The familiarity with local Indian place-names most likely occurred during the existence of the Portuguese colony in the area. The

Early Navigation

The mediaeval Irish monks, who pioneered navigation between the islands of the far North Atlantic, may have trusted in divine guidance to take them to their appointed destination. Undoubtedly, however, they were practical enough to have used other aids as well. We know that they kept records of the direction and distance (measured in sailing-time) to various destinations, and

offshore navigation must have been guided primarily by crude astronomical observations. They had no instruments to measure precise directions according to the sun and stars, or to gauge the altitudes of heavenly objects in order to calculate their position. Nevertheless, a practiced eye could probably steer fairly accurately by the sun or the pole star, and assess the north-south position quite closely by the elevation of these objects above the horizon and by the length of the summer night.

They must also have been guided by the many signs still used today by fishermen and other off-shore mariners who work from small boats: the direction of wind and wave, the colour and temperature of water, and the sea-life which is so apparent to small-boat sailors. Landfalls after voyages of longer than a day or two must have been largely dependent on such signs: shore-nesting seabirds, the

sea mammals which concentrate in the shallow water around islands, and weed or wrack from nearby beaches. When all else failed, a trust in God probably brought most mediaeval boats ashore, although probably often to different shores than those to which they were directed. Such voyages must have been the chief means by which new islands were discovered.

Sailors could find their latitude at sea by measuring the height of the North Star or the noon sun above the horizon. The mariners' astrolabe was a circular bronze plate with a scale engraved around the edge, and a bar with peep-holes (the alidade) mounted on a central pivot. In use, the astrolabe was suspended from a pivot, and the alidade rotated until the star could be seen through the peep-holes, or until the shadow of the sun lay directly along the edge of the alidade. The angle of the alidade was then read from the scale on the astrolabe.

The Norse who followed the Irish to Iceland, and then continued to Greenland and North America, did so with very little more navigational equipment. They had crude gauges of latitude, calculated by measuring the shadow of a pin mounted in the centre of a graduated disk, or the shadow of a gunwale across the thwarts of a boat,

and could probably maintain a fairly constant latitude in crossing the seas from east to west. Some have claimed that the Norse also used a *solarsteinn*, a small crystal of polarizing feldspar which allowed them to assess the position of the sun on cloudy days; such a piece of equipment was probably much less useful than would be suggested by the amount of argument over whether or not the Norse did use such stones. The Norse probably did not use charts, but probably had a mental picture of North Atlantic geography, augmented by verbal sailing directions. One set of such directions states:

According to learned men.... from Hern Island in Norway, one can sail due west to Cape Farewell

When tacking against the wind, a mariner used a traverse board to keep a record of distance sailed on each course. The board was a wind-rose, on which a wooden peg was placed for each half-hour of sailing in a particular direction. (Length: 40.8 cm)

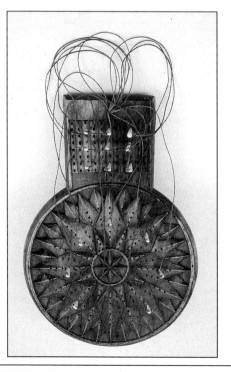

(the southern tip of Greenland), passing north of Shetland so far that you can just see it in good weather, and south of the Faeroes at a distance so that the sea appears half-way up the mountains, and south of Iceland at a distance that one sees only the birds and whales from it.

Such directions seem to have been quite adequate for crossing the North Atlantic from Norway to Greenland for four centuries or more. By the fifteenth century, when Europeans once again began to systematically explore the Atlantic, they did so with several navigational instruments which had recently been introduced. Most important was the compass, a magnetized iron needle floated in a bowl of water, suspended on a fine cord, or mounted on a pivot so that it is free to align itself with the magnetic field of the earth. The Chinese may have used magnets as divination devices or in geomantic calculations for several centuries, but the first known record of a magnetized needle being used for navigation at sea dates from only about A.D. 1100. The first European record of compass use appears almost a century later, and it is generally assumed that the instrument was introduced to Europe by Arabic or Persian traders from the Far East. Over the next couple of centuries, the Italians are given credit for developing a reliable and useful instrument from what must have been originally a generally erratic curiousity. Even sixteenth-century navigators had little understanding of magnetic declination (the variation between magnetic north and true north, which changes around the world and through time as the position of the magnetic pole changes).

Another introduction from the east was the astrolabe (an Arabic

*The astrolabe was originally an Arabic instrument, used by astronomers to study planetary motions and by astrologers to calculate horoscopes.
The astronomical astrolabe was much heavier and more complex than the instrument used by sailors.*

word and probably an Arabic invention). The astrolabe was the primitive forerunner of the mariner's sextant, but was a great improvement over earlier instruments. With patience and luck, a mariner could now calculate his latitude to within one degree (110 kilometres), and much of the early mapping of the New World was based on astrolabe sightings. By the late sixteenth century the astrolabe was being replaced by the more accurate cross-staff, a closer approximation to the sextant. Still, an astrolabe was carried by Samuel de Champlain on his explorations of eastern Canada. A small bronze astrolabe manufactured in 1603, which was found in the Ottawa Valley during the nineteenth century and thought by some to be Champlain's instrument, is now prominently displayed in the Canadian Museum of Civilization. In the well-known statue of Champlain on Ottawa's Nepean Point, the

explorer is sighting the sun through this astrolabe. Unfortunately for historical accuracy, he is holding the instrument at arm's length and upside down, as if using a sextant: astrolabes were suspended from a swivel, and held below eye-level.

Even with astrolabes and cross-staffs, early mariners had no method of precisely calculating their longitude — their position east or west of any other point. This had to be estimated from reckonings of ship speed and direction, and many early estimates were remarkably innacurate. This explains why, on many early maps, north-south measures are reasonably accurate, while there are major distortions in east-west directions.

Still, the development of maps and the accompanying rutters (lists of sailing directions from one point to another) were a major advance in the development of navigational abilities during the Age of Exploration. By the end of that period, cartography was becoming a precise science, and was beginning to develop the first recognizeable pictures of the world as we know it today.

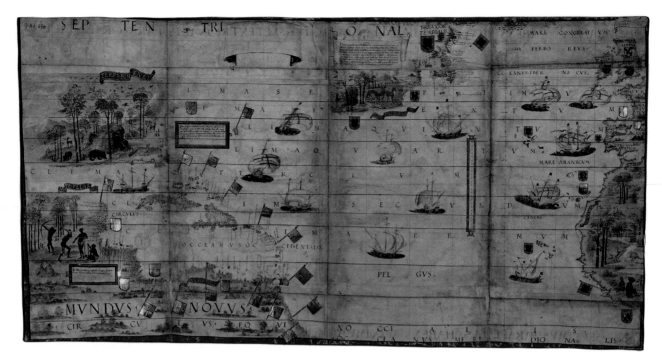

"beautiful bay" where the colony was located has confidently been assigned to various locales between the Strait of Canso and Ingonish on the northeastern coast of Cape Breton. I personally prefer Mira Bay, a pleasant inlet midway between what are now Glace Bay and Louisbourg, and the first large bay after the coast "turns north" at Cape Breton. It has also been suggested that one of the five early map names, *Xoracadie*, is derived from the Micmac name (Soolacadie) for Mira Bay. A pleasant summer could be spent searching the shores of Mira Bay for the archaeological remains of this first sixteenth-century colony in North America.

The Colony Abandoned

Wherever it was located, the Portuguese settlement on Cape Breton Island seems to have existed for only a few years. It was probably abandoned because of the hostility of the Indians who owned the local lands and turned out to be less submissive than first reported. One account states that, "Formerly the Portuguese sought to settle the land [Cape Breton]..., but the natives of the country put an end to the attempt and killed all of those who came there." Like the Norse attempt to establish a colony in

This section of a Portuguese atlas from 1519 records the explorations of the Corte-Reals. Above the coast of Newfoundland, which is not shown as an island, the inscription Terra Corte Regalis *is accompanied by two Portuguese flags. The legend at the left states that "Corte-Real passed through this region, first discovered it and gave it his name."*

Vinland five centuries earlier, and like Cartier's Québec colony 20 years later, or Raleigh's first Virginia colony 60 years later, the Portuguese could not maintain a European settlement in the face of native hostility.

With the loss of the Cape Breton colony, sixteenth-century Portuguese fishing interests seem to have concentrated on ship-based operations, working the offshore banks and sailing home with their salted catch. The "White Fleet" of Portuguese banking ships, whose periodic visits to the port of St. John's provided a notable tourist attraction until the past decade, are the descendants of these early efforts at fishing and exploration. The Portuguese trawlers which still work the Grand Banks are rusty reflections of a time when the Portuguese were the leading explorers and developers of Atlantic Canada.

CHAPTER 8

FROM ACADIA TO CAIN'S LAND

The French were relative latecomers to New World exploration. Yet two of their explorers, Verrazzano and Cartier, made important additions to the discoveries in the west. Their explorations opened the way to the interior of North America.

This sixteenth-century brass nocturlabe, or "star-dial," was used to calculate time at night. While viewing the North Star through the peep-hole, the observer moved the arms to coincide with certain stars in the constellations of the Little and Big Dipper. (Length: 25.5 cm)

thought to be either joined to the New Found Land or separated from it only by narrow straits, lay the Land of the Labrador and the ancient European country of Greenland.

The Spaniard Ponce de Leon had landed in Florida in 1513, in search of the Fountain of Youth placed there by Caribbean Indian tales, but Spanish exploration had extended no farther north. The English and Portuguese, who were primarily fishermen interested in the bounty of the Newfoundland and Nova Scotia fishing banks, had not ventured very far south of the Bay of Fundy. New Spain and the New Found Land were separated by about 15 degrees of latitude, over 1,500 kilometres. Were the two countries part of a single great continental landmass, or were they separated by an ocean through which one might sail directly to the Orient? Neither the gold-seeking Spanish nor the fishermen of England and Portugal had bothered to investigate this question, and the necessary exploration was finally undertaken by a mariner sailing from France.

Verrazzano's Voyage

French interest in the New World quickened in 1523, when the merchants of Lyons brought the navigator Giovanni da Verrazzano to the attention of the king of France. Like Columbus and Cabot, Verrazzano was an Italian and had probably learned the theory and skills of navigation in the schools of Italy. He had also gained considerable practical experience in Atlantic sailing from French ports, and had probably made at least one voyage to the Newfoundland fishing banks. His patrons saw in him a man who could explore and develop a direct westward sailing-route to Asia, a route in which other European kingdoms seemed to have lost interest at this time.

In order to accomplish this plan, Verrazzano was outfitted in the autumn of 1523 with a French naval vessel, *La Dauphine*, and three smaller ships chartered by his financial backers. After weathering a heavy storm, and engaging in some successful piracy against Spanish ships along the western coasts of Europe, the three merchant vessels turned back and only *La Dauphine* continued to the New World. The route chosen by Verrazzano was somewhat north of the one used by Spanish ships. He left land at the island of Madeira, and after sailing westwards into the Atlantic for about six weeks,

made landfall on the coast of what are now the Carolinas. He first sailed southward for a distance, hoping to explore as far as the known coasts of Florida, but at the same time wary of meeting Spanish rivals. Then, turning northwards, he began the long three-month voyage which would result in exploration of the entire eastern coast of the United States.

His first major discovery was a body of water that Verrazzano interpreted as a western sea, obviously the ocean which washed the shores of China, and separated from the Atlantic by a narrow strip of land only a kilometre or so wide. *La Dauphine* followed the shores of this isthmus for a hundred kilometres or more, anticipating but never finding a gap through which they could pass. The only geographical feature on the modern map which matches this description is the Outer Banks of North Carolina, a sandy isthmus stretching northward from Cape Fear to Cape Hatteras and beyond, and separated from the mainland coast by distances of up to 40 kilometres. Verrazzano's "Western Ocean" was nothing more than the shallow waters of Pamlico Sound, lying off the low and swampy coast of North Carolina.

Verrazzano's next discovery was a land of beautiful forests and handsome people, which he named "Arcadia" after the idealized pastoral countryside of ancient Greece. His crew marked their discovery of this wonderful land, inhabited by apparently peace-loving people, by kidnapping a child. The name Arcadia itself soon disappeared from New World geography, but was transformed by later mapmakers to "Acadie," and moved north to identify the early French settlements of what are now Canada's Maritime Provinces.

After sailing for some 400 kilometres along the low and generally featureless coasts from North Carolina to New Jersey, Verrazzano entered a broad and pleasant inlet fed by a large river, which can be confidently identified as New York Bay. After anchoring overnight in what is now the Verrazzano Narrows, and encountering Indians who appeared to be friendly, he continued northwards along the coast and next entered Narragansett Bay in what is now the state of Rhode Island. Here *La Dauphine* remained for two weeks while the crew rested, explored the surrounding countryside, and got to know the local Indians. The appearance and character of these people greatly

impressed the visitors, and there is no mention of further kidnappings.

Verrazzano's next encounter with Indians occurred on the coast of Maine, or possibly on the Atlantic coast of Nova Scotia, and was quite different: these people greeted the explorers with jeers and arrows. Although their language could not be understood, they were doubtless shouting that they had met Europeans before and had not appreciated their behaviour in kidnapping or pillaging harmless people. Verrazzano named this area the "Land of Evil People," and quickly left.

Another land was named by Verrazzano, but its location is unclear and known only from later maps, some of which extended it to in-

Fishermen from the French port of La Rochelle began to visit Newfoundland waters at an early date. In the late sixteenth century, the historian André Thevet even suggested that Rochellais ships had discovered Newfoundland as early as 1486. Exploring the Gulf of St. Lawrence in 1534, Jacques Cartier encountered a fishing vessel from this port.

clude all of the country from Cape Cod to the Gaspé. This land, under various spellings, was called something like "Norumbega." The name seems to have been derived from an Algonkian Indian language, and over the following decades it was elaborated by cartographers and armchair explorers into a city of great civilization and wealth, located somewhere in the hinterlands around the Bay of Fundy. However, Verrazzano cannot be blamed for the creation

The galleon was the workhorse of the sixteenth and
seventeenth centuries. Ships of this type served in voyages of
exploration, as cargo-ships in merchant ventures,
and in naval battles. They carried the gold and silver of
New Spain, as well as the whale oil and dried cod
of the New Found Land.

The galleon was an enlarged and improved version of the
caravel, with three or four masts and displacement ranging
from less than 100 tonnes to over 700 tonnes.
Its distinguishing characteristic was an inward inclination of
the upper hull, so that the deck was narrower than
the waterline width of the vessel. It could sail at eight knots or
more, and was a very seaworthy vessel although the high
stern-castle caused it to roll considerably. When armed
for combat or for protection against pirates,
it could carry over 50 cannon and remain stable despite the
great weight on the upper deck. For combat,
it could carry a crew of about 200 sailors and soldiers.

This model was inspired by an ex-voto in the maritime
museum at Madrid, dating from 1540, and by a sixteenth-
century Spanish document on shipbuilding.

1• Great cabin
2• Pilot house for the helmsman who handles
 the whipstaff
3• Tiller
4• Back pieces of the rudder
5• Gun room
6• Powder magazine
7• Well containing the bilge pump
8• Ballast
9• Keel
10• Gratings
11• Capstan to heave up or haul down the sails or
 mooring lines
12• Store room
13• Sail locker
14• Crew's quarter
15• Riding bitts
16• Ship's boats
17• Galley of the forecastle
18• Range of belaying pins
19• Bowsprit
20• Gammon lashing
21• Fore mast
22• Mainmast
23• Mizzen mast
24• Bonaventure mast

Florida and Cape Breton. Early Portuguese explorations in the vicinity of Greenland, as well as a probable English expedition to Arctic regions led by John Cabot's son Sebastian, had shown that any northern passage was probably blocked by ice-choked seas.

With areas to the north and south having been ruled out, the search for a passage to Asia was now concentrated in the mid-northern latitudes, around Newfoundland. Newfoundland waters were increasingly frequented by European fishermen during the early sixteenth century, but the geography of the area was poorly understood. Fishermen, of course, had little need or interest in mapping the New Found Land; all that they needed was a productive fishing ground, a convenient beach for drying

fish, and a clear sailing route home to Europe. Add to this the fogs and storms which characterize Newfoundland waters, and the nature of the coast itself — a confusing series of deep, wide bays, some masked or filled with numerous islands — and it is easy to understand why Newfoundland geography was a mystery in the early sixteenth century.

The first known French fisherman to work Newfoundland waters was Jean Denys, who sailed from the Norman port of Honfleur in 1506. According to an English description of the New World, written in verse about 1519, by that time over 100 French ships were making annual voyages to Newfoundland. By the 1530s the French were an important force in the Newfoundland fishery. As this fishery developed, some French fishermen — either more adventurous than their English and Portuguese rivals or, as latecomers, denied access to the best-known fishing grounds along the eastern and southern Newfoundland coasts — began to penetrate previously unfrequented waters. Although they left no records of early discoveries, we know that the first "official" explorers found French fishermen using the Strait of Belle Isle and the northern Gulf of St. Lawrence. It seems likely that the stories of these fishermen, telling of the great gulf "behind" the New Found Land, stimulated official French interest in exploring this potential passage through the New World. The mariner whom the French king chose to undertake this endeavour was Jacques Cartier.

Cartier's First Voyage

Jacques Cartier was a respected native of the Breton port of St. Malo, and was related by marriage to one of the principal families of that town. He was also related to an official of the nearby abbey of Mont Saint Michel, who secured his introduction to François I in 1532. Cartier, who was 41 years old at the time, was introduced as an experienced mariner who had already made voyages to both Newfoundland and Brazil. Although it is not recorded, the in-

troduction may also have suggested that Cartier knew certain secrets about a possible passage through the New World. Such a hint would explain why the king was so easily persuaded to support his first voyage of exploration; it would also explain why Cartier, having obtained the king's support, set an unhesitating course for the hitherto unrecorded Gulf of St. Lawrence.

The organization of a voyage required two years, but eventually the king provided enough money to outfit two small ships, each with a crew of about 30 men, with which Cartier left St. Malo on April 20, 1534. The route to Newfoundland was well known to sailors of Cartier's time, and the two ships made land 20 days later at Cape Bonavista. For the next five weeks, they sailed in known waters: first north in order to hunt great auks on the *Isle des Ouaiseaux* (Funk Islands) off the northeastern coast of Newfoundland, then northwest to the *Hable le Karpont* (Quirpon) on the northern tip of Newfoundland's Great Northern Peninsula, where they waited for ice to clear from the Strait of Belle Isle.

Entering the Strait in early June, Cartier described a number of harbours already named by French fishermen. Some of these names are

Verrazzano's Route

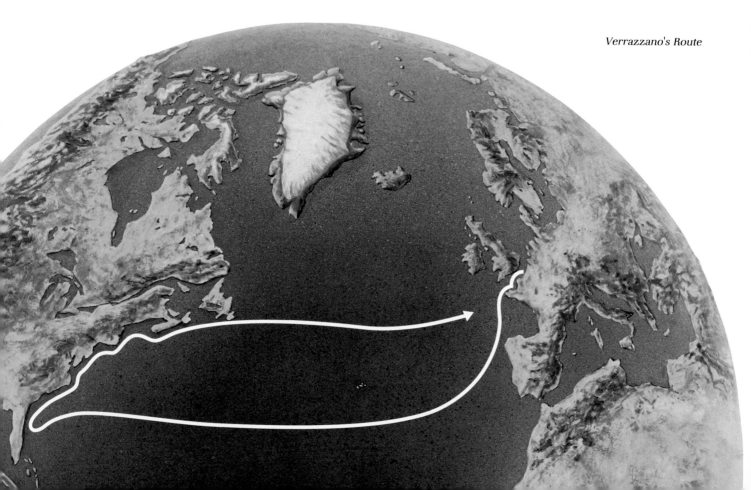

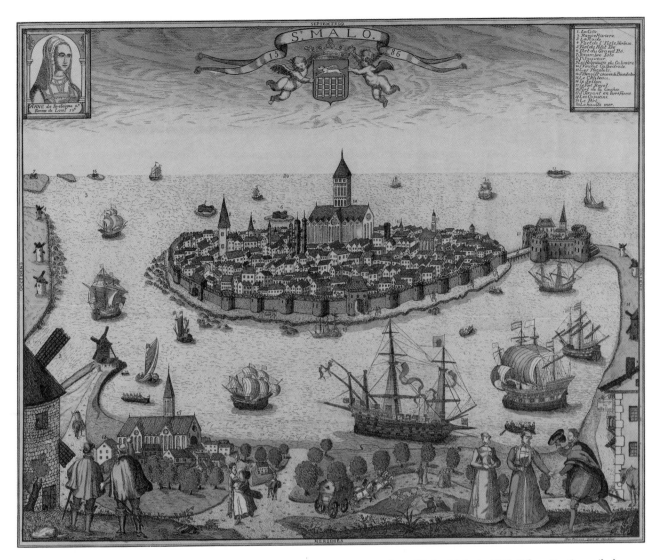

View of Saint-Malo in 1586. When Cartier sailed
in 1534, the town had about 5000 inhabitants.
For 15 or 20 years it had been a centre for
Newfoundland fishing ventures, and cod was an
essential part of the town's economy.
A document from 1519 states that fish were dried
on the shingle beach outside the walls.

retained today, from *Hable des Chasteaulx*
(Chateau Bay) in the north to *Blanc Sablon*, just
west of the present Québec-Labrador border.
Passing Blanc Sablon he visited two other
named localities: *les Islettes*, probably the present Brador Bay, where Cartier noted that there
was a considerable French fishery, and *Brest*
which can perhaps be identified with the present Vieux-Fort Bay.

Cain's Land

Having taken on wood and water, Cartier
continued west along a rocky, island-strewn
coast to which he began to apply names, apparently under the assumption that it had not been
previously explored. Despite his very unflatter-
ing view of the newly discovered country, which
he described as "the land which God gave to
Cain," he nevertheless took the time to set up a
cross as an assertion of France's claim of discovery. A few kilometres further to the west,
probably in the vicinity of today's Baie de

Jacques-Cartier, the explorers were surprised
to come upon a large fishing vessel from the
western French port of La Rochelle, an indication that the area was not as unexplored as they
had thought. By this time Cartier was well over
100 kilometres west of the Strait of Belle Isle,
and it must have been apparent from the state
of the swells and tides (if not from what he
learned from the Rochellais skipper) that they
were coasting the northern shore of a large
body of water lying to the west of Newfoundland.

Turning away from the northern shore of
the Gulf of St. Lawrence, Cartier struck out to
the southeast and soon reached the western

117

coast of Newfoundland. He followed this coast southward for a distance of approximately 400 kilometres, before heading westward to explore the Magdalen Islands, Prince Edward Island and the mainland coast of what is now eastern New Brunswick. In crossing the Gulf, Cartier was aware of the large swells coming in from the southeast, prompting him to note that there must be open sea separating Newfoundland from Cape Breton. These swells were, of course, coming through the 120-kilometre width of Cabot Strait. This strait may have been explored fifteen years earlier by the Portuguese Fagundes, or perhaps by Gomez, a Portuguese navigator sailing for the king of Spain who explored the coasts from Newfoundland to Florida the year after Verrazzano made his voyage.

Cartier may not have been aware of the earlier discovery of Cabot Strait, but there are indications that he knew he was not the first European to explore the area. The manners of the Indians encountered along the mainland coast, at some place in the Baie des Chaleurs, demonstrated that the European fur trade had preceded Cartier's exploration. These Micmac Indians approached the ship holding animal pelts on sticks, and indicating that they were willing to trade them for European goods. It has

Are we present at a kidnapping? We are at Gaspé on Friday, July 24, 1534. Cartier's sailors surround two frightened Iroquois boys, whom they have dressed in French clothing. These are the sons of Donnacona, whom Cartier is taking to Europe. Cartier tried to reassure their worried father "by showing them great signs of affection."

been suggested that the Micmac were not only used to dealing with European fishermen, but may have already begun to change their patterns of hunting to emphasize the taking of furs.

Another sign of earlier exploration appears a few days later when, approaching the eastern end of the Gaspé Peninsula, Cartier mentions a point of land named *Cap de Pratto*, either the present Cap Blanc or Cap Percé. The name "de Pratto" is unusual for two reasons; first, Cartier does not follow his usual practice of stating that he named the cape and explaining why he gave it this name; secondly, the name appears to be Spanish or Portuguese (probably *Cabo de Prado*, Cape Meadow) rather than French. This interpretation is supported by the fact that a French translation of such a name (Cap du Pré) appears on French maps dating a few years after Cartier's voyage. It seems likely that this portion of the Gulf of St. Lawrence had seen

Cartier's first voyage, 1534

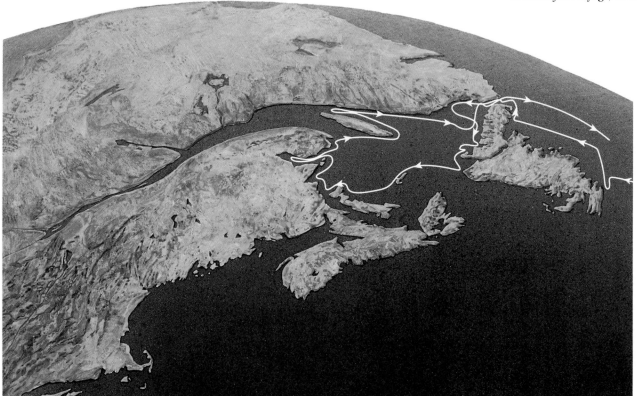

herited station in society, submission and obedience to those in higher stations, and a supposed duty to care for those in lower stations.

The Iroquoian political system, on the other hand, derived its organization and authority from the basic unit of society, the family. Inheritance passed through the female line, and newly-married men moved from their childhood homes to live with the families of their brides. The primary unit of Iroquois society was the group of nuclear families headed by a group of sisters, their daughters and nieces, who resided together in a single longhouse or in a certain area of a village, and all of whom were related through a single female ancestor. Most Iroquoian villages were composed of several of these extended family units. Each extended family elected two leaders (if the St. Lawrence people were like their Iroquoian relatives of New York State, the voters were the female members of the family and the chief was elected from a noble lineage): a civil chief who dealt with community and religious matters, and a war chief who organized and led the male members of the family in warfare. The affairs of each village were discussed by a council of the civil chiefs; decisions were reached by consensus of this council, and announced by a spokesman who was elected by the chiefs. The affairs of the nation were discussed by a similar council of village headmen.

Iroquoian society was based on the ideals of social equality, decision by consensus, and the absence of coercion: no individual or organization had the power to force another individual to live by a decision with which he did not agree. It has been argued that the concept of democracy, and specifically that form of democracy defined in the American constitution, was based to some extent on the Iroquoian model. We should not be surprised that Jacques Cartier had no awareness of Iroquoian social complexity. There was a similar lack of comprehension when the two systems of government — democracy and monarchy — met once again, 250 years later in Paris during the French Revolution.

Undoubtedly, Cartier had very little interest in comparative political theory. He was obviously aware, however, that the successful exploration and exploitation of the new country depended on maintaining civil relations with the occupying populations. He attempted to establish such relations in the traditional manner of a European dealing with the lower classes of his own land: by purchasing goodwill through the distribution of "goods of little value" (a phrase which recurs throughout his reports, as if he is afraid of accusations by his king or countrymen of paying too dearly for access to a new world); by a combination of bullying threat and stern rebuke; and by the judicious use of violence, up to and including abduction.

Such methods were far from the Iroquois ideal of politeness and non-coerciveness in human relations. Moreover, such methods could not force compliance from the men whom Cartier took to be "Captains" or "Kings," yet who lacked the authority which Cartier assumed them to have over their fellow citizens. As might be expected, Cartier's methods led to the gradual deterioration of relations between the Iroquois and the European newcomers.

We should not blame Cartier too harshly for the way he dealt with the Indians of the St. Lawrence Valley. He was a European of his generation, one that had also produced Cortes and Pissarro. Unlike the conquistadors of New Spain, however, Cartier lacked the support of an army, a fleet, and a monarch whose treasury was hungry for Mexican or Peruvian gold. With only the immediate support of his small crew, and the very distant and rather apathetic patronage of the French king, Cartier must have felt very isolated and extremely vulnerable among the Iroquois. The increasingly hostile relations between French and Iroquois cannot be blamed on the arrogance and ignorance of either side, but rather on mutual fear and suspicion. Such fears were the inevitable result of contact between two peoples who were totally inexperienced and naive at relations with others of different cultural backgrounds. Lacking both the experience necessary to deal diplomatically in a new cultural environment, and the military and administrative support necessary to win a new and populated land by force, Cartier's attempt to establish a French foothold in the New World was doomed to failure.

On Sunday October 3, 1535, Jacques Cartier and about 20 companions advance through fields of maize towards the Iroquoian town of Hochelaga, where the chief awaits his visitors.

Canada

Cartier's second expedition, with three ships and 112 men provisioned for a voyage of fifteen months, was considerably larger than the first one in 1534.

After making landfall at the Funk Islands and killing two boatloads of birds, Cartier proceeded to Blanc Sablon (at the modern boundary between Québec and Labrador) where he awaited the other ships of his storm-scattered fleet. By the time they had arrived, it was almost the end of July, very late in the season for exploration in unknown territory. Nevertheless Cartier set out westward, along the bleak and island-studded coast he had dismissed the previous year as "Cain's Land." Two weeks later he had reached the western limit of his previous explorations, and entered a small harbour which he named *baye sainct Laurens*; this name was gradually expanded by mapmakers of the following generation until it applied to the entire river and gulf explored by Cartier.

Cartier, however, was following other names, as he pursued a curious zigzag course up what is now the St. Lawrence River. Passing the western tip of Anticosti, which was finally recognized to be an island, he first steered southwestward toward the land which his captive Indian guides called *Honguedo*, the present Gaspé. The captives may have directed his course in the hope of meeting with a party of their countrymen, for they had been abducted from that same coast the previous summer. Encountering no Indians, however, they soon recrossed the narrowing river and began to explore the north shore. Now the guides assured Cartier that he was approaching the borders of the "Kingdom of Saguenay," whence came the copper that their people used as ornaments; furthermore, the river they had just crossed was "the great river of Hochelaga, and the route to Canada." By this time Cartier must have known, if he had not already known before he left France, that the passage to the west was a river of fresh water rather than a salt-water channel providing a passage through the New World to the Orient. Yet there is no indication that this realization changed his plans for westward exploration.

Having investigated the mouth of the present Saguenay River, and of other rivers along the north shore, Cartier continued heading up the St. Lawrence. In early September he eventually arrived at the Ile d'Orléans, in the territory which the captives called "Canada." Here they met a large party of Indian fishermen from the nearby community of Stadacona, which seemed to be the capital town of the territory. News of their arrival must have spread quickly, for the next day they were attended by a delegation led by Donnacona, the "captain" of the party Cartier had met the previous summer at Gaspé, and the father of Cartier's two captives. After a joyous reunion, and an exchange of gifts (fish, eels, maize and melons in return for the customary trinkets "of little value"), Cartier's men rowed their boats upstream and selected a harbour for their ships. Within a week the two larger ships, the *Grande Hermine* and *Petite Hermine* were safely anchored in the mouth of the St. Charles River at what is now the city of Québec.

Although the season was late, Cartier was determined on further exploration, and began preparations to set off upstream. He had learned that the Stadaconans had little of value, and was intent on penetrating the land of Hochelaga to the west, as well as learning more of the Kingdom of Saguenay. This plan was not what the Indians of Stadacona and Canada had expected. Insofar as they could understand the motives of the visitors, they may have believed that Cartier had reappeared solely in order to return the hostages, and to bring to their people the lucrative exchange of European metal goods for furs, a trade which other Europeans had already established with the Indians of the eastern seaboard. When it became apparent that Cartier was using their community merely as a stepping-stone in order to establish contact with more distant and wealthier peoples, they were understandably disappointed.

Cartier's first hint of trouble came when the two Indian boys whom he had taken to France the previous year (and who now began to be reported in the accounts of the voyage by their names, Domagaya and Taignoagny) refused to accompany him as guides and interpreters on his planned journey to the west. This may have been an attempt to persuade Cartier to remain at Stadacona, but it probably also reflected the simple and understandable unwillingness of the two boys — who had been staying well clear of Cartier's ships — to put themselves back into the power of the French. Discussions and negotiations continued over the next few days. The

The author of this 1556 map, Guillaume Le Testu, obtained much of his information from Portuguese documents. Most of the place-names are those given by Portuguese explorers, but French place-names in the Strait of Belle Isle demonstrate French penetration of the area. Cartier's second voyage is recorded in a series of names along the St. Lawrence River: Sept-Iles, Rivière de Saguene, Ille d'orléans, Ochelassa. The ornamentation of the map sustains the idea that, despite the recent setbacks of Cartier and Roberval, the New World was a land of promise.

Indians warned Cartier about the dangers of upriver travel, and arranged a shamanistic performance which resulted in a prediction that the French would perish from winter cold and snow if they proceeded upstream (a reasonably accurate prediction, as things turned out). Donnacona appears to have tried to conclude a formal alliance between Cartier and the people of Stadacona, first through the presentation of three children to live with the French, and later through the suggestion that one of his sons would accompany Cartier if a Frenchman were sent to live with the Stadaconans. Cartier interpreted the children as a gift, which he repaid with two swords and two washbasins. The exchange of hostages was refused, since by this time Cartier had lost all trust in the sons of Donnacona.

Leaving Stadacona on September 19, Cartier's small party travelled for almost two weeks up the St. Lawrence River. It was a slow but relatively uneventful journey, during which they passed numerous Iroquois camps and encountered a few Indian hunting and fishing parties. On October 2, travelling in two boats after having abandoned their small ship at Lake St. Pierre, they reached the shore of what is now the island of Montréal.

Hochelaga

Cartier's brief visit to Montréal provides one of the classic pictures of Canadian history. The scene is engraved in the mind of every schoolchild: the explorer is greeted as a visiting god, led through extensive fields of corn to a ceremonial welcome in the central square of the palisaded town of Hochelaga, and then to Mount Royal where he surveys the St.

129

Lawrence and Ottawa rivers extending — alas — into the heart of an unexplored continent rather than to an open Oriental sea. The actual scene is directly based on first-hand accounts, and is probably reasonably accurate. Yet in trying to reconstruct what happened on that October day, we must remember that Cartier, not trusting his previous hostages, had travelled to Hochelaga without an interpreter. Consequently, the underlying motives and emotions for the day's activities were probably far removed from those generally ascribed to the people involved.

It is very unlikely, for example, that the Europeans were mistaken for gods. The welcome Cartier received may have been little more than the one Hochelagan duty and politeness would have provided to any party of travellers newly arrived from a distant country. Lewis Henry Morgan, the early nineteenth-century student of the Iroquois, wrote that, "One of the most attractive features of Indian society was the spirit of hospitality by which it was pervaded. Perhaps no people ever carried this principle to the same degree of universality as did the Iroquois." The scale of the welcome probably also reflected the fact that Cartier's people were wealthy travellers who had access to rare and valuable artifacts: the manufactured metal objects which the Hochelagans had previously obtained only through trade with the peoples of the eastern seaboard.

On the European side, the actions of Cartier and his men must have been produced by a heady mixture of ambition, curiosity and fear. They were the first Europeans to penetrate any distance behind the eastern coasts of the northern New World. The Indian populations of the eastern coasts had little wealth of interest to Europe, aside from their fur clothing. Yet the Caribbean Indians who had been contacted by Columbus were also simple farming people, with little silver and gold. Only when Cortes penetrated the Mexican interior were the riches of New Spain revealed and acquired for Europe. Was it not conceivable that fifteen years later, a similar penetration of the northern New World would also reveal the existence of fabulously wealthy and fragile civilizations which could be exploited for the glory of France?

History has turned Cartier into a journeyman explorer, a competent but somewhat unimaginative man, who managed to complete a difficult task with little risk or excitement. This is certainly the impression which is gained by reading the first-hand accounts of his explorations. Yet his actions, as opposed to his reports (particularly the neglect of Stadacona, and the single-minded efforts to reach Hochelaga and to learn more of Saguenay) suggest that, in his heart, Cartier may have seen himself as a second Cortes. Given the geographical knowledge of the time, this was not a particularly wild delusion; gold mines, even forests of spice-trees, might well have existed in the upper St. Lawrence valley.

But if Cartier thought of himself as a Cortes, it was a Cortes who lacked an army, and who, consequently, was extremely wary of putting himself in the power of the native peoples of the New World. From what we can tell from his accounts, Cartier had not visited an Indian settlement before he reached Hochelaga. There is no indication, for example, that he had entered the town of Stadacona, off which he had anchored his ships. His previous dealings with natives had been either aboard ship, or in carefully arranged shoreline encounters where the numbers of Europeans and Indians could be roughly balanced, from which rapid withdrawal could be made by boat, and which were probably covered by his ship-board artillery. Now, somewhere near the present location of Montréal's Jacques Cartier Bridge, Cartier had reached his destination, Hochelaga. His two small boats carried 35 men, while on the shore there was a welcoming crowd which he estimated at 1,000 people. If he were to emulate Cortes and enter the capital city of this country, Cartier must leave his boats and put himself and his men at the mercy of the Iroquois.

The explorers chose to spend the night of October 2 aboard their boats, while the Iroquois gathered around fires along the shore of Montréal Island. A mid-October night (Cartier's dates are counted in the old Julian calendar, which is nine days ahead of the one used today) in a small boat on the St. Lawrence River must have been very uncomfortable, but we can hope that the weather was unseasonably warm. The next morning, Cartier arrayed himself in his finest clothing (some interpretations suggest that he wore armour, but this is unlikely), left ten men to guard the boats, and landed the remainder of his well-armed party. After advancing for several kilometres along a well-beaten forest road, they came to a fire where welcoming speeches were made by a headman. Cartier's party was then escorted through extensive cornfields to the town which he called Hochelaga. The town nestled against the slope of Mount Royal, and was home to approximately 2,000 Iroquois. The explorers were conducted through the single gate in the encircling palisade, and down a street between about 50 huge longhouses to a central open area. Here they found themselves among a massive but apparently quite orderly crowd of men, women and children.

In this setting, Cartier exchanged incomprehensible speeches (including a reading from the Bible) and gifts with the village headman, a paralyzed man about 50 years of age, and dis-

The first description of Hochelaga was published in Italian in 1556, by the celebrated Venetian editor Ramusio. The illustrator has attempted to include several episodes related to Cartier in this engraving: the town surrounded by a palisade, the fields of grain, the encounter with the chief etc. Unfortunately, the town plan seems to be based more closely on Italian Renaissance ideals than on New World reality.

tributed smaller gifts to the assembled crowd. Children and old people crowded around to touch the visitors, and the women laid out a feast in their honour. The French, however, refused to eat. They excused themselves to the Iroquois by stating that they were not hungry, and explained in their report that they did not like the taste of unsalted food. It is hard to believe that their tastes were so dainty, however, and they must have known that refusal to share food would be considered a great insult to their hosts.

Cartier and his men were probably suffering a mixture of disappointment and anxiety. They had entered the famous Hochelaga and found that it was not another Mexico, but a small farming town, whose chief wore a headband of porcupine quills rather than a golden crown. The people of Hochelaga considered shell ornaments to be their greatest wealth, and although Cartier investigated the shells, he found them to be of little value. Despite their poverty, however, these people had weapons and could easily overwhelm the French if the situation unexpectedly deteriorated. Under these circum-

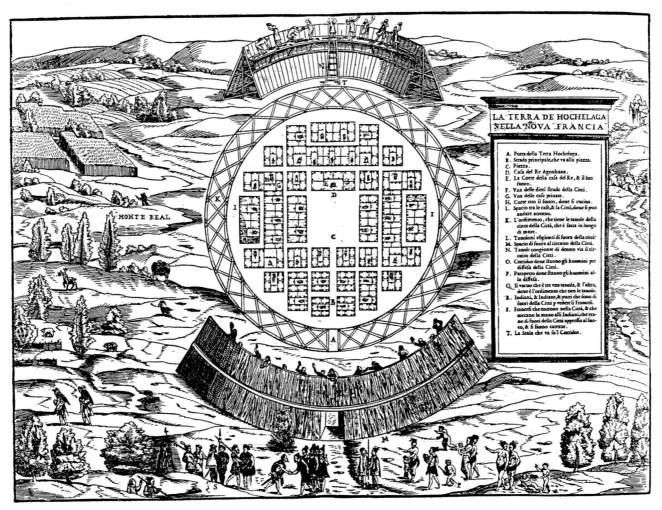

Charlesbourg-Royal, and the Search for Saguenay

Donnacona's stories of the Kingdom of Saguenay had the desired effect on the French king, who agreed to support a more ambitious effort at New World exploration. Cartier was to be in charge of recruiting a large number of settlers, from the prisons and elsewhere, and to use them to establish a permanent base of operations on the St. Lawrence. From this colony, major exploration efforts could be made into the interior. These plans were later changed so as to place a nobleman — Jean François de la Roque, sieur de Roberval — in charge of the project and representative of the king in the New World. Political, organizational and financial problems delayed the project until 1541. Even then, Roberval had not completed his arrangements; he found himself short of funds and decided to spend the summer in piracy. Accordingly, Cartier was ordered to set out for Canada in charge of a third expedition, five years after returning from his second.

Relatively little is known about Cartier's third voyage or the subsequent voyage by Roberval. The original French-language reports of the voyages are lost, and have survived only in the English translations summarized by the great sixteenth-century documentor of explorations, Richard Hakluyt. From these reports, and from other scattered documents and fragmentary references, we can reconstruct only the outlines of the two expeditions.

Cartier left St. Malo on May 23, 1541, with a fleet of five ships and a complement of gentleman-adventurers, soldiers, mariners, convicts and farm animals. They had a rough crossing, the ships became separated, and drinking water ran so short that the cattle, goats and pigs had to be fed on cider. The fleet eventually gathered in Quirpon Harbour in northern Newfoundland, took on water and wood, and sailed for Stadacona where Cartier had wintered five years before. They arrived on August 23, and were immediately met by a delegation from Stadacona asking about their long-departed relatives. Cartier, thinking that the new headman of Stadacona (who had been somewhat more pliant than Donnacona during the earlier stay) would be glad to have his position confirmed, truthfully reported that Donnacona had died in France. He lied about the others, explaining as best he could without an interpreter that they had remained in France "as great Lords, and were maried, and would not returne backe into their Countrey." The Iroquois "made no shewe of anger at all these speeches," but there were

Cartier's second voyage, 1535

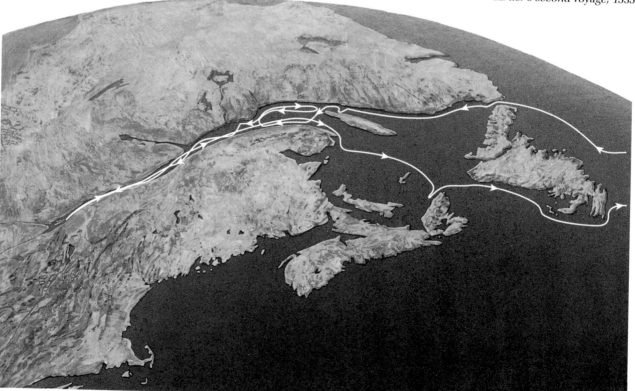

136

probably indications that all was not well. The account of the meeting goes on to report that the Iroquois show of contentment "was all dissimulation, as afterward it wel appeared." More significantly, Cartier immediately set out upstream to find a more isolated location for his colony.

The chosen site was apprxomimately fifteen kilometres further upstream, near the present Cap Rouge. Here he began to clear land and build a fortified post which he named Charlesbourg-Royal. Despite the lateness of the season they planted cabbages, turnips and lettuce, which sprouted in eight days but which must have soon succumbed to autumn frosts. They also prospected for minerals, and immediately found what they enthusiastically assumed to be great riches:

And upon that high cliffe wee found a faire fountaine very neere the sayd Fort: adjoyning whereunto we found great store of stones, which we esteemed to be Diamants. On the other side of the said mountaine ... is all along a goodly Myne of the best yron in the world, and it reacheth even hard unto our Fort ... And on the waters side we found certaine leaves of fine gold as thicke as a mans nayle.... And in some places we have found stones like Diamants, the most faire, pollished and excellently cut that it is possible for a man to see, when the sun shineth upon them, they glister as it were sparkles of fire.

Samples of the "diamonds" and "gold" were sent to France with two of the ships, along with news that the colony was established and preparing for the winter.

In early September, Cartier set out to reconnoitre the route he planned to follow the next spring to attain his main objective: the mysterious and wealthy Kingdom of Saguenay. His exploration party travelled in two boats, and followed the same route as his westward journey of 1535. They reached the present Montréal Island and left their boats in the same location as before. Rather than visit Hochelaga (which they now referred to by what is probably its true name of Tutonaguy) they continued along a portage trail upstream, to investigate the Sainte Marie and Lachine rapids. Here they encountered friendly Indian fishing parties, and were told of another major rapid located some distance upstream.

This bronze coin, bearing the arms of King Charles VIII of France (1483-1498), was found on the Gulf of St. Lawrence coast near Caraquet, New Brunswick. It carries the name of the city of Aquila, in central Italy, which was taken by the French in 1494. It may have been lost by a European visitor of Cartier's time, or before.

Cartier's visit to this heavily-populated section of the river was limited, as before, to a single day. By nightfall, complaining of not having eaten all day despite having been offered "Pottage and Fish" by the Indians, they returned to their boats, where they found a crowd of 400 people. The gathering was friendly, with a distribution of the usual "small trifles, as combs, brooches of tynne and copper, and other smal toyes, and unto the chiefe men every one his litle hatchet & hooke, whereat they made certaine cries and ceremonies of joy." The French continued to be wary, however, quickly setting off in their boats while noting that "a man must not trust them for all their faire ceremonies and signes of joy, for if they had thought they had bene too strong for us, then would they have done their best to have killed us, as we understood afterward."

This statement could well be taken as the motto for the remainder of Cartier's stay in Canada. He reached Charlesbourg-Royal to find that the local Indians were no longer trading fish to the inhabitants of the fort, but were suspicious and fearful of the French. The reputation which Cartier and his men had established five years previously, as well as the forsaken promise to return the kidnapped people who had been shipped to France, had taken their toll. The obvious intention of the French to establish a permanent colony on Iroquois land, without permission and without any obvious benefit to the Iroquois, must also have been taken as an insult and a threat.

Only scattered fragments of information survive to tell us what happened during the following winter at Charlesbourg-Royal. The Indians never made a decisive attack on the fort, but seem to have waged an effective guerilla war. They first killed a party of woodcutters in the nearby forest, and then others who ven-

Jacques Cartier ended his days at his small farm, named "Limoëlou", near Saint-Malo. The manor now belongs to the Macdonald-Stewart Foundation of Montréal.

tured from the fort; thirty-five Frenchmen are reported to have been killed. To those confined inside the fort, the winter must have been long and cold and miserable, aggravated by scurvy and other illness brought on by the absence of fresh food, and by the constant fear of attack. It is not surprising that by the following spring, Cartier had had enough of Canada. Soon after breakup, he abandoned Charlesbourg-Royal and set out down river.

Cartier must have followed his 1536 route homeward, through Cabot Strait and along the southern coast of Newfoundland. This time, however, he chose the harbour of St. John's to take on supplies before the Atlantic crossing. Here, by very unhappy accident, he met Roberval's fleet of three ships on their way to join his colony. Roberval ordered Cartier to turn around and return to Canada — probably the last place in the world that Cartier and his crew wanted to go. Accordingly, Cartier disobeyed his commander and slipped through the Narrows of St. John's harbour under cover of night. With a cargo of presumed gold, silver and diamonds that he hoped would offset the king's displeasure, he set a direct course for St. Malo. The cargo proved worthless, and Cartier's career as an explorer was over.

France-Roy

While Cartier was crossing the Atlantic for France, Roberval set sail for Canada by way of the east coast of Newfoundland and the Strait of Belle Isle. Cartier must have provided directions to his establishment, for Roberval sailed directly for Cap Rouge, landing there in late

July. Since there was no mention of Cartier's fort, we can assume that it had probably been destroyed either by Cartier or by the Iroquois. Roberval selected a nearby location and began to construct his own settlement, which he named France-Roy. It sounds like a more comfortable establishment than that of Cartier, with one of the two main sets of structures described as:

... a fayre Fort...wherin there were two courtes of buyldings, a great Towre, and another of fortie or fiftie foote long: wherein there were divers Chambers, an Hall, a Kitchine, houses of office, Sellers high and lowe, and neere unto it were an Oven and Milles, and a stoove to warme men in, and a Well before the house.

Despite the fort's amenities, the winter again proved long and miserable. Two ships were sent home before the river froze, and after they had left it was discovered that food supplies were going to run very short. Scurvy set in and about fifty people, perhaps one-third of the company, died. One man was hanged for theft, and others put in irons. There is no mention of hostilities on the part of the Indians, and in the spring they arrived to trade fresh fish in return for knives and trinkets. This suggests that Iroquoian animosity was not directed against all Europeans, but that it was specifically Cartier and his actions that had aroused their hostility.

In the spring of 1543, Roberval set out to attempt what Cartier had failed to do, and travel to the fabled land of Saguenay. With seventy men in eight boats, he set out upstream toward Hochelaga. Nine days later one boat returned, with the information that a second boat had been lost with eight hands drowned. Four days later, another boat arrived, carrying sixty kilograms of Indian corn, either stolen or purchased from a village on the route to Hochelaga. This is the last we hear of the journey to Saguenay, and we may suspect that Roberval, like Cartier before him, was discouraged from further exploration by the rapids and by the relatively dense Indian population of Hochelaga, the territory around what is now Montréal.

When Roberval returned to France-Roy, it must have been apparent that there was little advantage to staying longer in the New World. There is no record of the abandonment of the second colony at Cap Rouge, nor of whether he too collected a cargo of spurious diamonds and gold from the site, but we know that by early autumn Roberval was home in France. Of the eight shiploads of colonists who had followed Cartier and Roberval to Canada with hopes of riches and fame, the only person who was still alive in the New World was the young woman whom Roberval had abandoned on a desolate island in 1542.

Canada Abandoned

With the return of Cartier and Roberval, France abandoned her St. Lawrence River discoveries for over half a century. Winters were simply too long and cold, the native peoples too numerous and too willing to stand up for their rights, and the profits too meagre to maintain a successful European colony. The St. Lawrence had dealt the French too many disappointments. First seen as a possible waterway to the Orient, it had turned out to be a huge freshwater river draining an unknown continent. Still hopeful, the French went on to populate the continental interior with an unknown land, the Kingdom of Saguenay, rich in metals, stones and spices.

Belief in the fabulous Saguenay, a northern Mexico or Peru, died hard. Jacques Noel, Cartier's nephew and shipmaster, reported finding a map among the papers of his deceased uncle, with notes in Cartier's hand: to the west of Hochelaga, Cartier had written, "By the people of Canada and Hochelaga it was said, That here is the land of Saguenay, which is rich and wealthy in precious stones." To the south of this was another note: "Here in this Countrey are Cinamon and Cloves, which they call in their language Canodeta." Yet the belief in Saguenay was eventually killed by the hardships of the Lachine Rapids, and by common sense.

Finally, the rather pathetic efforts to dig gold, silver and diamonds from the very rocks on which he had built Charlesbourg-Royal, must have led to embarrassment, if not disgrace, on Cartier's final return to France. The King could no longer be interested in such a fiasco, and the St. Lawrence, like the rest of the New Found Land and the Land of the Bretons, was turned over to the exploitation of fishermen and whalers.

CHAPTER 10

THE GRAND BAY

The Labrador coast was the first region of North America to undergo extensive European exploitation. Recent archaeological work has recovered the remains of a sixteenth-century Basque whaling station, and a well-preserved shipwreck of the same period.

This iron harpoon head was lost by Basque whalers at Red Bay in the Strait of Belle Isle, and was found in a pond on Saddle Island at the mouth of the Bay. The letter "M" was perhaps an owner's mark, to identify the harpoon if it was carried away by a wounded whale (Length: 40 cm).

The Strait of Belle Isle, the narrow northern entrance to the Gulf of St. Lawrence, is a meeting place of the arctic and temperate zones. From the north comes the cold Labrador Current, carrying icebergs from Greenland and the pack ice that often fills the Strait until early summer. From the south flow the warmer currents of the Gulf of St. Lawrence, bringing nutrients gleaned by the rivers draining from the Great Lakes and much of eastern Canada. Both the currents and the abundant sea life they support are funnelled through the narrow waters of the strait.

Some of the best salmon rivers of the Atlantic coast are found along these shores, vast shoals of capelin roll on the beaches each summer, and cod are plentiful. Massive herds of harp seals whelp on the spring ice after wintering in the gulf, then move northward through the strait to their Arctic summering grounds. In earlier times, herds of grey seals and walrus hauled out on local beaches, and large numbers of whales navigated the open waters of summer.

Humans have long known about the productivity of the Strait of Belle Isle. About 9000 years ago Indians had occupied the area, and by about 7000 years ago, they were living so well that they could afford to build a large burial mound at L'Anse Amour. About 3000 years ago the place of the Indians was taken by Palaeoeskimos from the north, who brought their Arctic hunting skills to bear on the area's rich sea-mammal resources. The Straumfjord (Current Fiord) of the Norse sagas — location of the short-lived Vinland colonies — was probably the Strait of Belle Isle. Five hundred years later, John Cabot's exploration of 1497 probably brought him to the general area, where he reported cod so plentiful that they could be caught by dipping baskets over the side of the ship. By the time Jacques Cartier explored the strait in 1534, European fishermen had already named many of the bays and harbours, and for the remainder of the sixteenth century the strait was one of the most heavily exploited areas of North America.

Although this exploration of the area has long been known to historians, few details of the sixteenth-century European occupation of

The tryworks consisted of a stone foundation containing several ovens, each of which supported a large copper cauldron. From a wooden platform, men fed the cauldrons with whale blubber, then drew off the rendered oil to be cooled in tubs of water.

The costume of this Basque sailor consists of a knitted cap, shirt, jacket, breeches and tailored wool stockings. One of the burials excavated from a peat bog at Red Bay was dressed in this fashion; the waterlogged acid soil had dissolved the skeleton but had preserved woolen clothing.

the strait could be found. Most of the early European visitors to the area — fishermen, whalers, traders and occasionally pirates — had a vested interest in keeping secret the source of their valuable cargoes, and they quite understandably left few records. Only during the past decade has a combination of archival research and archaeology begun to reveal something of the nature of one of the more organized ventures: that undertaken by Basque whalers from northern Spain.

A Discovery in the Archives

The first detailed information about the early whale-fishery in the Strait of Belle Isle was found by Selma Barkham, an archival researcher employed by the Public Archives of Canada. Barkham searched the archives of several towns and cities in the Basque region of northern Spain, and in poring through thousands of notarial documents — contracts, wills, lawsuits, promissory notes, insurance claims etc. — she found a number relating to the whale fishery in the "Grand Bay." The Grand Bay was the sixteenth-century name for the Strait of Belle Isle, and some of the locations mentioned can be located fairly precisely because they have kept their sixteenth-century names to the present day: the Basque *Xateau* became the French Baie des Chasteaux and the present Chateau Bay located just north of the strait; the Basque *Semadet* became St. Modeste, and the site of the recent settlement of East St. Modeste at the mouth of the Pinware River.

Archaeological confirmation of these and other Basque shore stations mentioned in the records was desirable, and in the summer of 1977 Barkham arranged to make a brief visit to the southern Labrador coast, along with James Tuck, an archaeologist from Memorial University of Newfoundland who had spent several summers researching the prehistoric occupations of the Strait of Belle Isle area. At several locations they found beaches and gardens littered with fragments of the red roof tiles that the Basques had imported for their structures. They also found a few structural remains which may have dated to the Basque occupation of the area.

Red Bay

The 1977 findings were so interesting that Tuck decided to return the following summer in order to excavate the most promising site, one located on Saddle Island in Red Bay. Red Bay is one of the finest harbours in the Strait of Belle Isle, and from old documents and maps it can probably be identified with the harbour of *Buttus*, one of the principal Basque shore stations. Saddle Island forms a plug in the mouth of the bay, a small treeless island aptly named for the hills at either end. On the harbour side of the island, several fragments of old stone walls were stained with a black material, which was identified as burnt whale oil. Excavation

The illustration shows the activity of a Basque whaling station in the Strait of Belle Isle around 1580. After having towed the whale ashore with capstans, butchers climb over the carcass and remove the blubber in long strips which are lifted by a crane. On the working stage, other men cut the blubber into cubes which are rendered to oil in large cauldrons. Cooled and purified, the oil is poured into barrels and towed behind boats to the waiting ships.

proved the walls to be the remains of the ovens where whale blubber was tried into oil, the most important product of the whale fishery at that time.

The largest of the oven areas consists of a stone wall ten metres long, one metre wide and over one metre high; on the shore-side, offshoots from the wall separate five fireboxes in

The cooper and his helpers were charged with assembling and repairing the barrels that would be used in transporting whale oil to Europe. Prefabricated in Europe, the barrels were disassembled to save space on the trip to Labrador. The photograph shows a complete barrel recovered in pieces from the wreck in Red Bay.

Whales and Whalers

Over 30 species of whales occupy, or at least visit, the waters off Canada's coasts. These include playful human-sized porpoises and dolphins; the small white beluga and the unicorn-tusked narwhal of Arctic waters; the elegant and deadly killer whale; and the massive sperm whale which feeds on giant squid taken from the depths of the ocean. All of these species are "toothed whales" with rows of peg-like teeth which are used to capture fish or (in the case of the killer whale) sea mammals and other whales. Fortunately for these creatures, the Industrial Age has never found a major use for their bodies. The products which are taken from these whales — beluga skin for the Inuit diet; narwhal tusk for the ivory and curio trade; killer whales for aquarium entertainment; and the teeth, spermaceti and ambergris of the sperm whale — have not justified an all-out hunt to the death of the species.

The whales which have suffered most from human industry are the "baleen whales," creatures as large as the blue whale that can attain a length of over 30 metres and a weight of over 140 tonnes. Unlike the toothed whales, these animals feed entirely on tiny shrimp-like crustaceans called "krill," which float throughout the seas and are concentrated in northern latitudes. Baleen whales live by filtering the krill from sea-water through great panels of baleen, a tough, flexible plastic-like material which hangs in curtain-like rows in their mouths. They

Until recently, Portuguese whalers from the Azores hunted whales from small open boats. This photo was taken in 1975.

swim more slowly and are more easily captured than toothed whales, yield vast amounts of oil and meat, and the elastic baleen has found numerous uses as springing for nineteenth-century carriages and upholstery, as the "whalebone" of corsets, and even as springs for wind-up toys.

In the early days of whaling, efforts were concentrated on two closely-related northern species, the North Atlantic right whale and the Arctic bowhead. Besides yielding huge amounts of whale oil and baleen, these animals are slow-swimming and docile, easy to approach and harpoon from a small boat. More importantly, they float when killed. Because of these characteristics, they soon became known to early English whalers as the "right" whales to pursue, and the name has stuck. The English, however, were latecomers to the art of whaling.

The large baleen whales of the Atlantic Ocean were initially hunted by two very different peoples. The first were probably the Inuit of Arctic Canada, who arrived on the fringes of the North Atlantic about A.D. 1000, bringing with them the techniques of whaling which had been developed in Alaskan and North Pacific waters. The Inuit hunted whales from skin-covered "umiaks" up to 10 metres long, using large toggle-headed harpoons carved from whale bone

or ivory, attached to a line carrying floats or drags which would impede the escape of a struck whale. About the same time, and certainly before A.D. 1200, the Basques of the Bay of Biscay coasts began to develop a similar hunt from wooden rowing boats about the same size as the Inuit umiak, using barbed iron harpoon heads attached to a line with wooden drags to slow the whale.

During the sixteenth century, these two whaling peoples met on the coast of Labrador. By the end of that century, the whaling effort at stations such as Red Bay had proved so effective in depleting northwestern Atlantic whale stocks that it put an end to both the Basque Labrador fishery and the Inuit whale fishery in the eastern Arctic. In the following centuries the Basques became the harpooners and mentors for the Dutch and English whaling fleets which preyed on newly discovered populations of baleen whales in Greenland and Spitsbergen waters. When these whales had been hunted

North Alaskan whalers hunted whales from large skin-covered boats called umiat. *The Eskimos of southern Alaska hunted whales from kayaks, using lances smeared with a poison derived from aconite.*

out, the Inuit extended their traditional whaling techniques to become harpooners and contract-hunters for the Scottish and American whalers who began to penetrate the ice-covered waters of Arctic Canada during the nineteenth century.

The Arctic hunt was over by the beginning of World War I, with the depletion of the final bowhead populations of the North Atlantic. From their summer feeding grounds off Labrador, to the High Arctic "nursery" grounds which were finally reached by the steam-driven whaleships of the late nineteenth century, the bowheads were hunted to near-extinction over four centuries. The bowheads and their relatives, the sadly-named right whales, are among the rarest of sights off Canada's coasts today.

which the oil had been tried in large copper cauldrons. The fireboxes were built of sandstone, probably brought from Spain as ballast. The Basques must quickly have learned, as Tuck did by experiment, that the local granite soon crumbled in a hot fire. Fragments of copper in the fireboxes are probably evidence of more spectacular problems, when cauldrons broke and released up to 200 litres of flammable whale oil into the fire below. On the inner side of the wall, opposite the fireboxes, are the remains of a wooden platform from which men fed blubber into the cauldrons and ladled out oil to be cooled and clarified in tubs of water. A layer of tiles over the entire feature indicates that the structure had been roofed. Five such structures were found along the eastern shore of the island, two of them associated with the remains of stone and timber wharves or slipways where the whales had been flensed.

During 1978 and in the following years, Tuck and his team went back to Red Bay, each year locating more evidence of Basque activities. Three structures, marked by broken roof tiles in large rectangular patches measuring up to 8 by 14 metres, are obviously the remains of houses or workshops. From these came fragments of pottery and glassware, a coin minted in Toledo during the reign of Philip II, a key, a rosary, knives, adzes, the tongue of a wood-

A model of the whaling ship was built on the basis of information recovered by the underwater excavations. This shipwreck has considerably increased our knowledge of galleons, and of sixteenth-century naval construction.

working plane, a portion of a saw blade, and other artifacts. The presence of woodworking tools suggested to the team that these buildings were coopers' shops, where the barrels used to ship whale oil were constructed. This was confirmed when a boggy area beside one of the shops was excavated and found to contain waterlogged and well-preserved barrel parts and the refuse of barrel-making. The glassware and pottery, as well as several personal belongings recovered from the cooperages, were of considerably better quality than those found around the oven areas, suggesting that the coopers had a higher standard of living than did the men who flensed the whales and stoked the ovens. This is not surprising, considering that the safe transportation of whale oil from the Grand Bay to Europe depended on the skill and care of the coopers.

The hearths and animal-bone refuse suggest that the coopers may have lived in their shops, which were comfortably roofed and upwind from the tryworks. Other small hearths are scattered over the island, generally in small sheltered nooks between outcrops of bedrock; the presence of occasional potsherds, and fragments of baleen (possibly used to roof these tiny shelters) suggest that these may have been the cramped, smoky and very uncomfortable sleeping places of the other men who worked at the station.

Sunken Ships

Evidence of another important part of the whaling operation came to light in 1978, when

An archaeologist works on the wreck of a Basque whaling ship, found in 1978 close to Saddle Island. This could be the San Juan, *which was driven aground in a storm in 1565, while fully loaded with whale oil and ready to leave for Europe. Hundreds of barrel staves and heads were found in the wreck.*

Robert Grenier of Parks Canada led an underwater survey of the area and discovered the well-preserved remains of a sunken ship only 30 metres offshore from the Saddle Island station. In subsequent years Grenier and his team of underwater archaeologists excavated portions of the 300-tonne ship, recovering its compass, anchor, capstan, transom, rudder, and a loaded swivel gun. The wreck was littered with thousands of barrel staves and heads identical to those found ashore, and those in the midship area were so little disturbed that it was possible to reconstruct how the barrels had been stacked in the hold.

A trench excavated between the wreck and the shore station showed a continuous layer of wood chips, artifacts, and whale and codfish bones, indicating that the wreck and the shore station were contemporaneous. We may even know the name of the ship and the date of its sinking. Records of a lawsuit found by Barkham in Spanish archives refer to a ship named the *San Juan*, which in late 1565, fully loaded with whale oil and ready to sail for Europe, was blown aground in Buttus harbour and sunk with no loss of life. Although it is impossible to prove that the wreck is the *San Juan*, the identification seems plausible. In any case, the work of Grenier and his team has recovered not only evidence of another aspect of the Basque whale fishery, but also important information on poorly known sixteenth-century naval architecture.

Whaling in the Grande Baie

The combination of Barkham's archival research, Grenier's underwater investigations, and Tuck's dig on Saddle Island has put together a remarkably complete picture of the early Basque whale fishery in southern Labrador.

In the spring of each year during much of the late sixteenth century, ships like the one

Capitalism, Discovery and Exploitation

The successful exploration and exploitation of the New World did not simply grow out of the maritime abilities which Europeans had developed by the sixteenth century. These ventures certainly depended on the seaworthy vessels and navigational abilities of the period. However, they were also dependent on the growth of commercial structures which allowed the concentration of capital needed for distant exploration, and which also permitted the reliable and efficient distribution of profits among the investors in such enterprises.

The Irish monks who traversed and made discoveries across at least a portion of the North Atlantic during the Middle Ages, did so as individuals simply searching for a place to live a life of poverty and contemplation. The Norse who followed in their wakes had greater ambitions, but little means to bring about their fulfillment; they were led by local chieftains who had little backing other than their own strength and authority, and whose only wealth came from farming marginal lands or from Viking raids in foreign territories. Neither

Lyon was a financial and commercial centre whichplayed an important role in transatlantic discovery. Verrazzano's voyage of exploration was financed by the Florentine and French bankers of the city.

the Irish, the Norse, nor any other mediaeval Europeans could have assembled the human and financial support needed to establish a successful colony or base of exploitation in North America, or even to undertake significant exploration of the continent.

During the centuries which separated the voyages of Eirik the Red and Columbus, Europe underwent a vast social and economic change from a mediaeval continent where wealth and power was measured in land, to a mercantile society in which monetary power was the basis of national and royal might. The change was pioneered

by the cities of northern Italy, who were the primary beneficiaries of the twelfth and thirteenth-century Crusades to the Holy Land. Not only were Italians contracted to transport crusaders and supplies to the Middle East, but they were the first to gain a foothold in the trade which the Crusades opened with the countries of the Orient. In 1252 Florence issued the gold "florin," the first gold coin to be widely traded in Europe for 500 years, and soon emulated by other "great coins" issued in Italy and elsewhere. The simple existence of a valuable and widely-recognized currency, instead of the small silver coins which in earlier times had

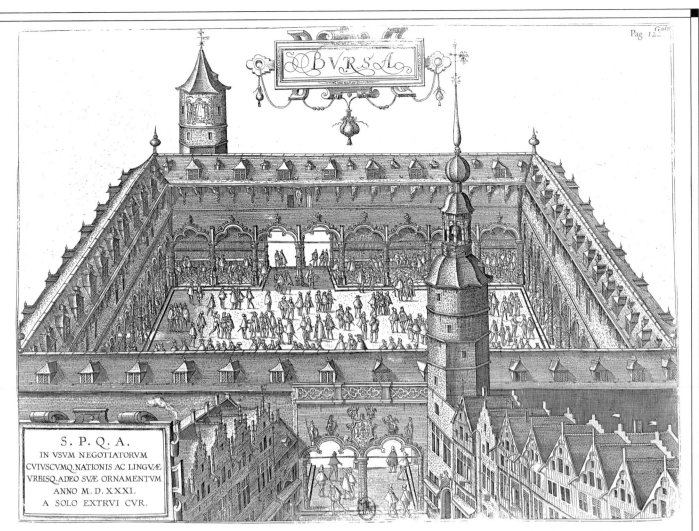

BVRSA

S. P. Q. A.
IN VSVM NEGOTIATORVM
CVIVSCVMQ. NATIONIS AC LINGVÆ
VRBISQ. ADEO SVÆ ORNAMENTVM
ANNO M. D. XXXI.
A SOLO EXTRVI CVR.

been traded largely by weight, was one of the necessary prerequisites for the efficient expansion of trade.

The development of banking systems also facilitated the growth of commerce and trade. By about 1275 the city of Siena had become the banking centre of Europe, later to be overtaken by Florence whence the Medici bank established branches throughout the continent. With the establishment of such banks, merchants could make payments across Europe through paper transfers rather than the physical transfer of coin, and could safely invest the profits of their enterprises. The twelfth- and thirteenth-century onslaught by the Church against usury, the collecting of interest on money loaned, probably reflects a widespread employment of the practice. The campaign against usury had little effect, since usury was not against the laws of

Judaism, nor of Byzantine and Syrian Christianity. Roman Christians habitually disguised interest payments as gifts, bonuses or rates of exchange on investments made in a foreign currency. Throughout the period, there was an apparent growth in investment and in the availability of credit, which in turn facilitated the growth of trade.

Other developments which allowed the expansion of overseas trade and the exploitation of overseas resources included contracts of partnership, between the investors who backed an enterprise and the shipowners or captains who undertook the venture; insurance contracts, or loans which had to be repaid only if the venture was successfully concluded; and risk-sharing schemes in which several investors held shares in a vessel and in its voyage. For ventures which required considerable manpower, such as fishing, whaling or

During the Age of Discovery, Antwerp was a leading European financial centre, and its stock exchange attracted bankers from many countries.

piracy, a system of payment was developed whereby each officer and crew member was paid a fixed share in the profits of the voyage.

From the pioneering ventures of Columbus and Cabot, all New World voyages of the sixteenth century had a commercial motive, whether it was the opening of trade with the Orient, the pillaging of New Spain, or the plunder of the fish and whale resources of the New Found Land. Their successful organization and achievement depended as much on the newly-developed European techniques for concentrating, manipulating and investing capital as on the increase of maritime skills and technology.

151

found in Red Bay set sail from northern Spain bound for the Grand Bay, loaded with rock ballast, barrel heads and staves, food supplies, and whaling gear. On their arrival at the shore station, structures that had been damaged during the previous winter were repaired by the voyagers, using local timber and imported roof tiles. The hunters then rowed out into the strait in their small whaling shallops (the remains of two such boats were found in the underwater excavation) in search of the slow-swimming right and bowhead whales.

The whales were harpooned (an iron harpoon point 40 centimetres long was found in a pond on Saddle Island) and killed with lances, then laboriously towed back to the station and grounded at one of the slipways. Men with long flensing knives stripped the blubber from the whale, which was then towed from shore and allowed to sink or to wash ashore in Red Bay, where in places the shores are still littered with whale bones. The blubber was cut into chunks and carried to the tryworks, where the oil was rendered over fires of wood and blubber.

Meanwhile the coopers were repairing barrels and constructing new ones from parts brought from Spain. Filled with oil, the barrels were rolled to the beach and towed out to the

This illustration of a whale hunt is placed in the vicinity of Iceland on a Spanish map of 1413. The presence of a bishop on the ship also recalls the legend of St. Brendan.

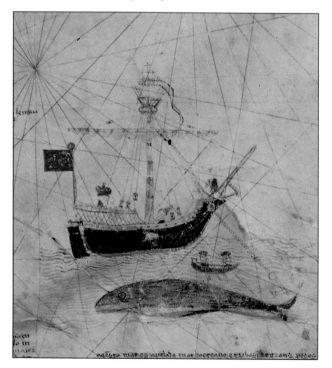

ship anchored offshore. When whales were scarce and work slow, the men devoted their time to jigging for cod, which were split and dried either for their own use or, more likely (to judge from the large number of cod bones found on the bottom just off the station) as additional cargo for Europe. At other times, when several whales had been towed to the beach, the trying furnaces must have flared through the night. By late autumn the ship's holds would have been filled with casks of oil (the *San Juan* had 1,000 barrels aboard when she sunk) and bundles of dried fish, with the crew anxious to begin their slow passage home before being caught by winter ice.

Such a successful voyage was very profitable for the owner of a whaling ship; in 1571 one cargo of oil was insured for a value equal to that paid in the same year for the purchase of two large galleons. The whalers, coopers and other workers were paid on a share system, and must have received enough to attract them year after year to a hard life on this cold coast so far from their homeland. Occasionally the men paid with their lives for the opportunity of working in the Grand Bay. The worst misfortune, other than a sinking, was to be caught by the early formation of winter sea ice, forcing a winter stay in Labrador. The archival documents mention several such events, some of which resulted in deaths from cold, hunger and scurvy. Tuck's unexpected discovery, in 1982, of ten skeletons on Saddle Island may relate to one such occurrence. The men had apparently been laid out on the ground surface instead of being buried, indicating that their deaths had probably occurred during the winter when the ground was frozen. The fact that they had not been buried during a subsequent whaling season suggests that they may have died toward the end of the Grand Bay whale fishery, late in the sixteenth century. Many other burials have since turned up, over 140 in all, consisting of individual and mass graves, and one case of 12 or 13 bodies which were simply tossed into a pit, perhaps the record of another overwintering disaster.

The Whalers
Disappear

The end of the whale fishery in the Strait of Belle Isle was probably due to a combination of factors. The intensive hunting of the previous several decades almost certainly brought about

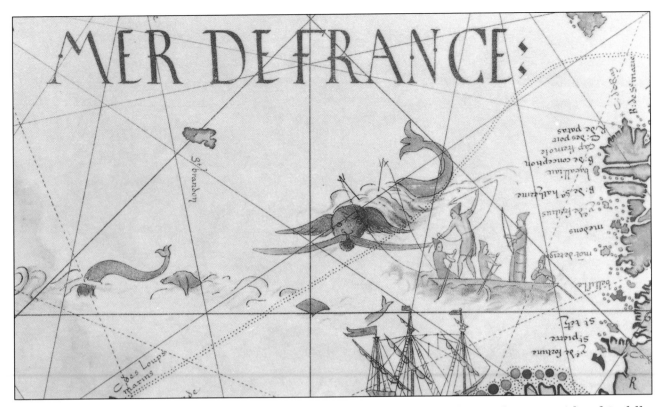

The cartographer Pierre Desceliers drew this picture of whalers near the Strait of Belle Isle on his map of 1546. This is the earliest illustration of whaling on a map of the New World.

a decline in the local whale stocks, making hunting more difficult. An upsurge in Dutch, French and English privateering in the North Atlantic at that time probably caused some problems for the whalers, and many of the whaling ships were commandeered and lost in the Armada sent against England in 1588. Also, at about that time there were reports that French fishermen in northern Newfoundland and the Gulf of St. Lawrence were suffering attacks from local Indian populations, and perhaps from Inuit who may have begun to travel south from their northern Labrador homeland in order to trade with or plunder European fishermen. During the following centuries several accounts tell of the depredations of the Inuit, including the burning of unattended boats and shore stations in order to recover iron nails, which could be refashioned into useful artifacts. In 1986, Tuck excavated a number of hearths on the west side of Saddle Island; around them were scattered the stone tools used by local Indians of the time, as well as nails and other artifacts that had come from the Basque station, probably plundered in the early spring before the Basques returned for the summer hunt.

Whatever the cause, by the early seventeenth century all that remained of the Grand Bay whale fishery were the records of contracts and lawsuits scattered through the archives of northern Spain, a few sunken ships, and the crumbling stone walls, broken roof tiles and the bodies of dead whalers slowly being covered by the turf of the southern Labrador coast. Yet from these remnants it is possible to construct at least the outlines of one of the earliest European occupations of the New World. In very characteristic European fashion, this occupation was an industrial enterprise. Also characteristically, it probably resulted in the virtual destruction of a local resource — the whale population of the northwestern Atlantic.

CHAPTER 11

META INCOGNITA

The sixteenth century saw Elizabethan England emerge as a leading naval power. One of the Queen's most notable mariners was Martin Frobisher, whose search for a Northwest Passage to Asia led to the first English establishment in the New World: a mining camp on the barren rocks of Baffin Island.

This arquebus, an early portable firearm supported by a prop and braced against the chest, dates from about 1580. It is probably of the type used by Frobisher's men against the Inuit (Length: 132 cm).

For over four centuries, Europeans have sought a sea route across the northern edge of the North American continent. Although such a route was actually discovered during the last century, fewer than three dozen passages have been made to date. The route is not commercially practicable even with current marine technology. With ice-breaking tankers and freighters now being designed, the dream of the Northwest Passage may become a reality in the coming decades. Powered by massive engines, their path through the ice fields scanned by radar and satellite cameras, these huge ships will be designed to move through the heaviest ice conditions of the polar seas.

It has taken 400 years to develop a technology capable of subduing the ice of the Northwest Passage sufficiently to permit commercial sea traffic across the top of the continent. The crews of these ships of the future, working in a climate-controlled bridge and plotting their course and position with electronic instruments, will rarely have occasion to examine the shores of the channels through which they pass. However, in the distance they may occasionally glimpse the marker-cairns and other remains left by earlier, unsuccessful attempts to locate and navigate a Northwest Passage.

The first such voyages to leave a permanent mark on the Canadian landscape were those of

Canada's first gold rush occurred in 1577, when the explorer Martin Frobisher's search for a Northwest Passage was diverted by the discovery of a rock sample thought to contain gold. The find encouraged two ventures to Baffin Island in 1577 and 1578. The 1578 endeavour included 15 ships and 400 men, and was the largest Arctic expedition ever assembled.

Martin Frobisher in the years 1576 to 1578. Frobisher's expeditions grew out of the rapid expansion of English sea power and oceanic trade which occurred during the reign of Elizabeth I. The Elizabethan period is still revered as a "golden age" of English culture and enterprise. It was an age in which the finest products of the European Renaissance finally reached England, changing the country from a feudal state into a mercantile nation. New continents, new theologies, new insights into the natural world and human society, were subjects of wide public interest, and they were rapidly transforming the English view of the world. So much poetry was being written — Shakespeare was only the first

This map shows "Frobushers Straightes" leading to "Cathaia" (China) across northern North America. These straits provided a short and easy route to the Orient according to George Best, one of Frobisher's captains who published the map in 1578. The map was probably drawn by James Beare, principal surveyor of the Frobisher expeditions. The name Meta incognita *identifies a group of islands at the entrance to the strait.*

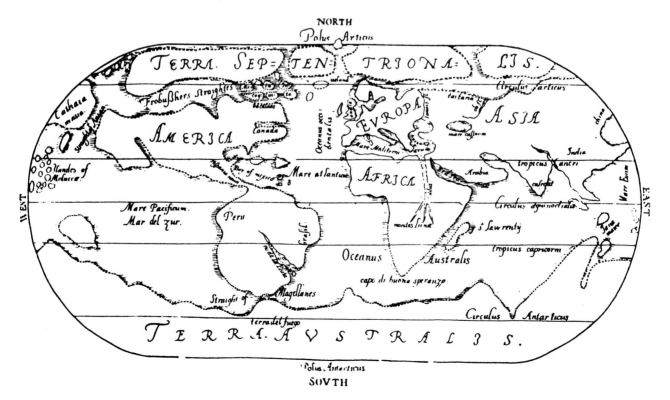

156

FRANCIS BACK 90

decisions, including the one that allotted all newly discovered continents to either Spain or Portugal. As a boy of fourteen, Martin Frobisher survived one of the first English ventures into Portuguese territory, an expedition to obtain spices and gold from West Africa; it returned vast profits, but left more than two thirds of the crew dead of fever in the African summer. Ten years later, as the result of another interloping trade expedition, he spent a few months as a prisoner in a Portuguese fortress in what is now Ghana. Frobisher's African experiences may have led him to look for healthier work in colder climates. He spent some time as a sucessful privateer, sometimes veering into piracy since he is known to have looted at least one English cargo. By the 1570s his name was associated with a scheme for the discovery of a "Northwest Passage" to the Orient, a scheme which also involved the illustrious Sir Humphrey Gilbert and other notables.

Gilbert was, in fact, the author of a tract which was published in order to attract interest in Frobisher's venture. Using all recognized geographical knowledge, both ancient and recent, Gilbert concluded that the continent "commmonly called America" was "an Iland environed round with Sea": to the south was the Strait of Magellan, on the west the Mar del Sur (South Sea, now the Pacific), and on the east the West Ocean (Atlantic). Finally, to the north, was "the sea that severeth it from Greenland, thorow which Northern Seas the Passage lyeth, which I take now in hand to discover." He saw a Northwest Passage as a means by which England could take the lucrative Oriental trade from the Spanish and Portuguese, whose southerly routes were proven, but long and expensive. England would gain a monopoly on goods found in lands yet undiscovered, and could use "some part of those countreys" to settle "such

among many of almost equal talent and productivity — that one suspects that the people of the time generally conversed in blank verse. There was little distinction between the poet, scientist and the man of action, or between actions in the fields of private enterprise and state policy. The latter distinctions were no more blurred than in the fields of maritime commerce, where privateering intergraded with piracy, and where mercantile endeavours were closely tied to political aims.

English ventures into the newly discovered worlds of the sixteenth century can be seen as an indirect result of the marital habits of Queen Elizabeth's father, Henry VIII, which brought about his break with the Church in Rome. As a result, England was no longer bound by papal

needie people of our Countrie which now trouble the common welth, and through want here at home, are inforced to commit outragious offences, whereby they are dayly consumed with the Gallows." Gilbert's tract is a curious forerunner of the colonization proposals that would become common in the British Isles two or three centuries later, and which resulted in a considerable part of the early settlement of eastern Canada.

The Northwest Passage

The search for a Northwest Passage was not new in Frobisher's time. John Cabot was looking for such a passage when he made his 1497 discovery of the New Found Land. Some of the Portuguese voyages, which resulted in the re-

discovery of Greenland about 1500, may have been stimulated by hopes for a route to Asia. However the reports which these expeditions brought home, if they returned at all, were of nothing but storms, barren, rocky lands and ice-covered seas. Sebastian Cabot, the son of John and a man who gained a reputation for reporting voyages that never took place, may have made an expedition to what is now Labrador in 1508, and he may have entered Hudson Strait. Another voyage, sailing in 1527

In entering the bay which now bears his name, Frobisher's men encountered a number of men "in small boates made of leather." This engraving, imaginatively portraying a group of Inuit, was based on information from the Frobisher expedition. The man in the kayak is hunting birds with a barbed dart propelled by a spear-thrower.

under the Bristol master John Rut, seems to have been aimed at the eastern Arctic but, after the first view of sea ice, headed southwards and ended in the Caribbean. Aside from these few voyages, Europe seems to have lost interest in a Northwest Passage through Arctic waters very early in the sixteenth century.

Why, then, was the idea revived much later in the century? The new interest may have been aroused by casual, accidental and unrecorded voyages to the far northwestern Atlantic. As we have seen in earlier chapters, by mid-sixteenth century the fishing banks off the Newfoundland coast had been heavily populated by French, Portuguese and Spanish fishermen. The Basque whaling fleet was intensively working the waters off the southern coast of Labrador. Trading for furs with the native peoples of eastern Canada was an increasingly lucrative sideline to many fishing and whaling voyages, and encouraged ventures to previously unfrequented coasts. The Inuit whom Frobisher encountered on Baffin Island had iron-tipped weapons, and seemed to have been in recent contact with Europeans — perhaps fishermen or whalers strayed from the fleets working the Labrador Sea to the south. Tales of new lands, or of newly discovered westward-leading channels sighted by lost or storm-driven mariners,

may have been reinforced by remnant knowledge of the Norse geography of Greenland and adjacent areas.

In sixteenth-century Scandinavia, there appears to have been continued interest in the fate of the Norse colonies of Greenland, which had been out of regular contact with Europe for over a century. A crusade was mounted in 1520 to regain Greenland from the heathen, but it never set sail. The twentieth-century explorer Vilhjalmur Stefansson, who carefully edited and analyzed the reports of Frobisher's voyages (and who knew by first-hand experience the importance of vague hints in directing an explorer's course of action) thought it likely that Frobisher not only knew where he was going, but also knew the actual sailing directions preserved from Norse times in Greenland. These sailing directions came originally from the report of Ivar Bardarson, the Church official who had been sent about 1350 to learn the fate of the Western Greenlandic Settlement. This report was available in a German translation by 1560 and, Stefansson thinks, was probably circulating in the original Latin at least a century earlier. The availability of such documents may have stimulated Frobisher's interest, and that of other Englishmen, in revisiting the once-known lands and seas of the far northwest.

Frobisher's Routes

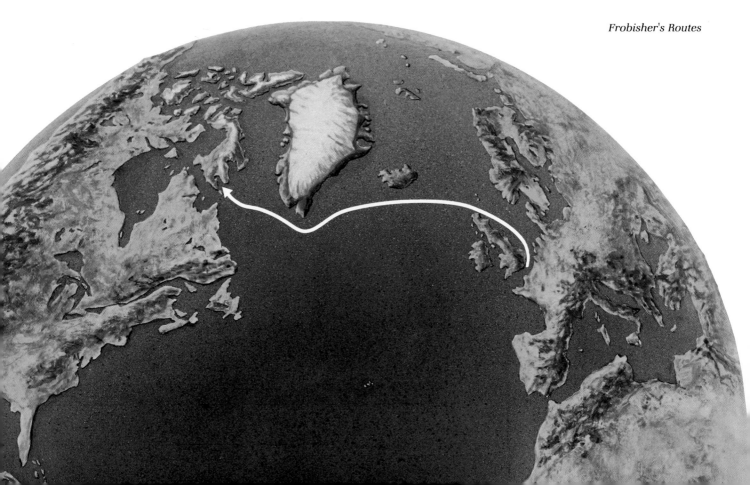

Frobisher's First Voyage

Frobisher's first voyage was organized and financed by certain merchants of London, with the assent of the Queen and a licence issued by the newly-formed Muscovy Company. A small ship, the *Gabriel*, was built for the voyage; a somewhat larger vessel named the *Michael*, and a tiny pinnace for inshore work, were purchased. These ships may have reflected Frobisher's experiences in privateering, where small and fleet ships capable of running through inshore waters were often at an advantage. All three ships were certainly smaller than the vessels used by Columbus, Cabot, Cartier, or any of the early transatlantic venturers whose ships we know, and were manned by a total crew of only 35. The ships were outfitted with the latest in maps, texts on geography and navigational instruments, and supplies, including 600 litres of aqua vitae.

This is one of the two large mines dug in Kodlunarn Island. In the course of two expeditions, 1,500 tonnes of rock were quarried from the area, at the cost of 40 human lives.

The small fleet left London in early June, Queen Elizabeth waving farewell from a window at Greenwich. Soon after leaving the Shetland Islands, they met a storm and the small pinnace was lost with all four hands; ships of this size were generally carried on the decks of larger vessels, and Frobisher was probably unwise to have tried to sail his across the North Atlantic. Two weeks later, they were off the east coast of Greenland, where the *Michael* turned back in sea-ice and storm, reporting that Frobisher's ship had been lost. This report was either mistaken or untrue, for Frobisher's remaining ship and its crew of 18 men sailed around southern Greenland and on to the west, where they discovered a high rocky country which they named "Queen Elizabeth's Foreland" (the present Resolution Island).

The Archaeology of Maps

Long before the first European ship appeared along the eastern coast of the New World, every cove and creek and sandbar of that coast was already named in a local aboriginal tongue, from the Inuit language of the Arctic to the Yahgan language of Tierra del Fuego. Very few of these names survived to appear on modern maps. One of the privileges of a European explorer was to give names to the geographical features he encountered, and few explorers ever gave a thought to the fact that these features were already named.

Most explorers took the procedure of naming quite seriously; Jacques Cartier, for example, conscientiously noted in his journal the reasoning behind most of the names which he applied. They usually referred to the explorer's patrons, the saint on whose day the feature was discovered, a peculiarity of the feature itself or an event that occured at the time of discovery. The names were almost always given in the language of the explorer, or in that of his royal patron if they differed. The history of exploration can therefore be traced in the languages of the place-names on various coasts.

The earliest European place-name which still survives in the New World is "Greenland," the name given by Eirik the Red to attract settlers to his new country. No other Norse names survive in the regions west of Iceland; although the sagas and other records tell us of many mediaeval Norse place-names in the New World, the knowledge of their locations died out with the Norse Greenlandic colonies. Similarly, there are no surviving place-names which originated from John Cabot's or other early English explorations of the east coast; again, Cabot disappeared before the placenames which he undoubtedly gave were transferred to maps or to the knowledge of local residents.

There is little doubt that the earliest European placenames which survive and continue in use today are Portuguese. These names are concentrated along the eastern coast of Newfoundland, where they appear on charts from the early 1500s as well as on the most recent road maps, good evidence of continuous local occupation since the time when the names were given. The most prominent names include Cape Race (*Cabo Raso*, "Cape Shorn"), the prominent cape at the southeastern tip of Newfoundland, probably named for its treeless tundra vegetation; Cape Spear (*Cabo da Espera*, "Cape Hope") just south of St. John's harbour; Conception Bay (*Baia de Cocepicion*) with Baccalieu Island (*Ylha dos Bacalhaos*, "Codfish Island") in its mouth; Cape Bonavista (*Cabo de Boaventura*) and Fogo Island (*Ylha do Fogo*, Island of Fire). A few names along the south coast of Newfoundland may also derive from early Portuguese originals, such as the deep bay now marked on maps as Bay d'Espoir; the local pronounciation from which this spelling was derived is "Bay Despair," and was more likely derived from the early Portuguese *Baia de Espera*.

In northern Newfoundland and the Strait of Belle Isle region, the place-names reflect early French rather than Portuguese use. Such names include Quirpon (*Karpont*); Chateau Bay (*Hable des Chasteaulx*); and Blanc Sablon, names which were already in use when Cartier entered the Strait in 1534. Several of Cartier's Gulf of St. Lawrence place names also continue in present use. Again, the survival of these names indicates continued use of the Strait of Belle Isle and of some portions of the Gulf of St. Lawrence for the past five centuries. Aside from Cape Breton (from the Portuguese *Cabo de Bretones* "Cape of the Bretons," or less likely "Cape of the English"), neither the Atlantic coast of Nova Scotia nor the coasts of New England shows placenames dating to the earliest period of exploration. For example, none of the place-names given by Verrazzano during his extensive explorations from the Carolinas to Nova Scotia, have survived.

The study of place-names seems to indicate that only one

area of eastern North America has seen continuous use by Europeans since the time of early sixteenth century exploration: the Atlantic coast from Cape Breton eastward around southern and eastern Newfoundland and northward to southern Labrador. The Portuguese names along most of these coasts, together with the French names in the Strait of Belle Isle and the Gulf of St. Lawrence, form a history of the region engraved in geographical knowledge, maintained by continuity of European occupation and folkloric tradition.

Such a continuity of tradition is shown in only one other region of eastern North America. On eastern Baffin Island, several modern place-names (Loks Land, Countess of Warwick Sound, Frobisher Bay etc.) are those given by Martin Frobisher in the 1570s. The land discovered by Frobisher was lost to history for 300 years, and the "Frobisher names" have been re-applied only during the past century, so they cannot count as evidence of continuous use. Yet in the midst of these English names, modern maps show the tiny "Kodlunarn Island" as the site of Frobisher's most extensive mining activity. The name, meaning "White Men's Island" in the Inuit language, indicates the continuity of Inuit occupation of the area, and the accuracy of Inuit historical traditions, over the past four centuries.

After considerable trouble with ice, they eventually sailed to the west into a long, narrow body of water which they named "Frobisher's Streytes," and which they believed separated Asia to the north from America to the south. The idea that such a narrow channel could penetrate to the South Sea was based on an analogy with Magellan's Strait at the southern tip of South America. That narrow and tortuous channel winds between high snow-covered mountains for 200 kilometres before granting access to the Pacific. Frobisher probably hoped that the American continent tapered to the north as well as to the south, and presented a similar channel to the northern Pacific ocean. Being an experienced mariner, however, he must eventually have begun to find that the tides and currents were not those of an open strait, but resembled those of an enclosed bay. He was sailing the length of what is today known as Frobisher Bay.

Having proceeded "60 leagues" to the west in his newly-discovered "strait" (actually a distance which cannot have been much more than 150 kilometres), Frobisher came upon the first inhabitants of the country. From the top of a hill, he "perceived a number of small things fleeting in the Sea a farre off, whyche hee supposed to be Porposes, or Ceales, or some kind of strange fishe; but comming nearer he discouered them to be men, in small boates made of leather." Over the next few days Frobisher developed a familiar relationship with the Inuit who came aboard the *Gabriel* with meat and fish, traded sealskin coats and bearskins for bells and mirrors, and competed with the sailors at acrobatic games in the ship's rigging. Their apparently easy acceptance of the newcomers, as well as their possession of iron, has been argued as evidence that the Inuit had had previous dealings with Europeans.

These friendly exchanges were brought to an end by a curious incident: five of Frobisher's men used the ship's boat to carry a visiting Inuk back to shore, and neither men nor boat returned. Frobisher assumed that the men had been captured by the Inuit, but lacking a boat to go ashore, he could do little about it. They sailed close inshore, fired a cannon and blew trumpets, and waited to no effect. The Inuit were now wary of the ship, but one was finally enticed close enough that Frobisher could grasp him and lift man and kayak aboard, holding him hostage. This produced no results in

This sparkling black stone is the principal ore sought by the Frobisher expeditions. It is a piece of gneiss from Kodlunarn Island, and contains no traces of gold or any other valuable mineral.

the way of an exchange of prisoners, and Frobisher eventually gave up on his five men. With only 13 men left, barely enough to handle the ship, and finding 30 centimetres of snow on deck one morning, the captain headed home for England. No evidence of the five lost men was to come to light during his subsequent expeditions to the area. Three centuries later, however, the Inuit of Frobisher Bay told another story. The five had been marooned by Frobisher; they had built a boat and sailed away the following summer, but had been lost in the ice.

Frobisher returned to England without having proven the existence of a Northwest Passage, but apparently optimistic that he had sailed partway through such a passage. He brought home the captured Inuk and his kayak, "which was a sufficiente witnesse of the Captaines farre and tedious travell towardes the unknowne partes of the worlde." He also brought back certain objects "in token of Christian possession," which had been gathered from an island where his men had landed while waiting for ice to clear from the straits. Among these objects was a black stone which looked like coal, but which was so heavy that it might contain metal. This piece of rock became the centre of a strange story: it was given as a souvenir to the wife of one of the venture's backers; she, for an unexplained reason, threw it into the fire, and then retrieved it and quenched it in vinegar, at which it "glistered with a bright Marquesset of gold."

The rock was taken to an assayer, who confirmed that it was indeed a very high-grade gold ore. Tales of comparable complexity and credibility traditionally circulate around the discovery of deposits of precious metals; one is reminded of the hammer thrown at a fox,

which revealed the rich silver deposits at Cobalt in northern Ontario. Nevertheless, to a company which had operated a money-losing venture such as Frobisher's, the story was a great and unexpected asset. On its basis they received a royal commmission to make a voyage in order to bring home gold ore, as well as sufficient investment to clear their debts and mount a new expedition.

The Second Voyage

In the spring of 1577, Frobisher's backers formed the Company of Cathay, in order to exploit his discoveries of the year before. Queen Elizabeth herself invested 1,000 pounds, a greater sum than the total which had been collected for the first voyage. The two small ships used the previous year were now joined by a relatively huge naval ship, the *Ayde*, with a complement of 120 sailors, soldiers, gentlemen, goldfiners and miners. Frobisher's primary instructions were to mine a cargo of gold ore; only if he could do so without interfering with the mining operation was he to conduct further explorations of his "strait."

The trip across the North Atlantic was less stormy than that of the previous year. Once again they coasted the shores of Greenland without being able to land because of ice, then crossed to Baffin Island, which had now been named by the Queen *Meta Incognita*, the Unknown Land. Here, on the highest hill of an island now named Loks Land after Frobisher's principal backer, the party erected a large boulder cairn (which still stands) and took possession of the country in the name of Queen Elizabeth. On their way back to the ships they encountered their first Inuit of the voyage. After some friendly trading, the English tried to capture two Inuit as further hostages. This incident ended with one Inuk captured, an Inuit arrow in Frobisher's buttock, and a bad beginning to his attempts to recover the Englishmen lost the previous year. Several days later a more desperate skirmish occurred, in which five or six Inuit were killed, one Englishman gravely wounded, and a woman and a baby kidnapped.

There were other encounters with the Inuit, including one at the mine site on what Frobisher named "Countess of Warwick Island." At this meeting, the captive man was allowed to talk to his compatriots, and explain that the Inuit hostages were being held in order to be exchanged for the five lost Englishmen. A letter, pen, ink and paper were sent with the visiting Inuit, but with no result. Having given up on finding his men, Frobisher now seems to have lost heart for further exploration. As stated in the account of his Lieutenant, George Best, "considering also the shorte time he had in hande, he thought it best to bend his whole endevour for the getting of Myne, and to leave the passage, further to be discovered heereafter. For his commission directed hym in this voyage, only for the searching of the gold Ore, and to deferre the further discoverie of the passage untill another tyme."

A fortification was quickly thrown up to protect the selected mine-site from surprise attack, and the company set about the business of quarrying and loading ore. By August 21, the ships had been loaded with 200 tonnes of rock, the sea was beginning to freeze, and Frobisher decided to set out for home. Within a month the ore was being unloaded in Bristol and at Dartford on the Thames, where smelters had been built for the refining process. Two different German assayers had been hired, and each pronounced that the ore was so rich that the voyage had made a considerable profit. Plans were immediately laid for a third and much

Kodlunarn Island lies at the mouth of Frobisher Bay in southeastern Baffin Island.
The two large trenches excavated by Frobisher's miners show clearly in this aerial photograph.
In the Inuttitut language,
Kodlunarn means "White Men's Island."

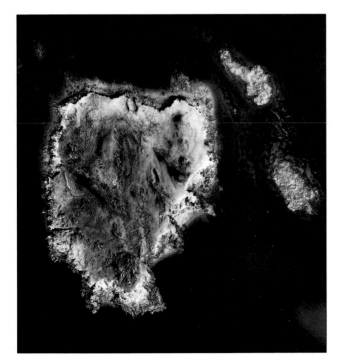

larger venture to take place the following year. The three Inuit captives, like their predecessor of the year before, died within a month of reaching England.

From our distant vantage point, there is a fascinating and ominous similarity between the patterns of Frobisher's exploration and those of Cartier forty years earlier: the growing numbers of kidnapped natives, the gradual realization that a passage to the Orient had not been found, and finally, the discovery of precious metal in great abundance. The final element of the pattern — the revelation that their ore was worthless — would not become clear for another year.

The Third Voyage

The search for the Northwest Passage was now almost forgotten in the lure of easy gold. The 1578 venture, comprising 15 ships and 400 men, was the largest Arctic expedition ever mounted, before or since. Yet this was not a genuine voyage of exploration but an industrial venture that happened to take place in an Arctic landscape. It was also an effort at colonization. Perhaps harking back to Sir Humphrey Gilbert's tract on the resettlement of the English poor in newly discovered lands, the ships carried materials to build a small settlement, and eighteen months' supplies for the 100 men who would be left in *Meta Incognita*.

The fleet set sail on May 31, following the same route as that of the preceding summers. This time, however, they managed to land on the southern coast of Greenland, taking possession of it under the name "West England." Here they examined some abandoned Inuit tents, finding a box of small nails, an "iron tryvet" and "dyvers other things artificially wroughte, whereby it appeareth that they have trade with some civill people, or else are in deede themselves artificiall workemen." By July 2 they had crossed Baffin Bay to the mouth of Frobisher Bay, which they found choked with ice. A storm at the edge of the ice-fields caused great distress to the fleet, and sank the ship carrying most of the building materials for the proposed settlement. Regathering after the storm, Frobisher mistakenly led the fleet into what is now Hudson Strait, proceeding for some distance before he realized his error and returned. The ships eventually gathered in late July at the Countess of Warwick Island, and the business of mining ore was begun. By late August, over 1,300 tonnes of rock had been loaded into the vessels of the fleet, from mines on the island and along neighboring coasts.

During a conference of the captains, which brought to light the fact that there were neither materials nor supplies sufficient to establish a settlement, it was decided to abandon this portion of the plans. Nevertheless, a single house was built, to see if it would withstand winter snows, frost, and vandalism by the native inhabitants. For the benefit of these people, and to encourage their future friendship, the house was furnished with "dyvers of oure countrie toyes, as belles, and knives, wherein they specially delight.... Also pictures of men and women in lead, men a horsebacke, lookinglasses, whistles and pipes. Also in the house was made an oven, and breade lefte baked therin, for them to see and taste." Barrels of provisions were buried for use by an expedition planned for the following year. In an excess of optimism, the men planted peas and grain "to prove the fruitfulnesse of the soyle against the next yeare." After sermons and ceremonies, the fleet departed fully laden for England, where they all arrived safely in early October.

No one returned the following year to harvest the grain and peas, or to dig up the provisions and investigate the state of the house. There were no further voyages to *Meta Incognita*, since it soon transpired that the "gold ore" was nothing but valueless rock. Frobisher was disgraced, and the location of his new land was lost to memory for almost 300 years. Its rediscovery was based solely on archaeological evidence.

Frobisher's mines were not found until 1861, when the American explorer Charles Francis Hall was shown their location by the Inuit of eastern Baffin Island. On a small island known as Kodlunarn, at the northern entrance to what is now Frobisher Bay, Hall described finding two great trench excavations, as well as the ruins of a house and workshop. This find was confirmed in 1974 by the late Walter Kenyon, an archaeologist with the Royal Ontario Museum in Toronto.

An Elizabethan Settlement on Baffin Island

In preparing to mark the 400th anniversary of Frobisher's voyages, Kenyon and a small crew spent two weeks on Kodlunarn Island. He investigated the ruins of Frobisher's "house", a structure measuring only 2.5 by 3.5 metres with thick walls of rubble masonry, as well as the remains of a larger building which appeared to be a blacksmith's shop. The remains of campsites, work areas and stone-quarries were scattered around the island and on nearby shores. Kenyon writes, "It still seems strange to me that Hall could find traces of Frobisher's smaller camps still visible after the passage of 300 years, and that I could find them just as easily after another 100 years."

The archaeological sites on Kodlunarn Island are Canada's best-preserved remains dating to the Age of Exploration. They represent a heroic episode from our past, the first attempt to plant an English colony in the New World. Isolated as they are at the far eastern tip of the Arctic Islands and 150 kilometres from the nearest settlement, the sites are vulnerable to casual scavenging or more organized looting. These sites should be preserved, protected to the best of our ability, and passed to future generations. The ethic of conservation must be extended to include unique and fragile archaeological sites that few of us will ever have the opportunity to see, yet which remain important witnesses to our past.

CONCLUSION

In the thousand years between A.D. 600 and 1600, Europe underwent remarkable changes. At the beginning of the period, the decline of the Roman Empire was still felt on a continent in which power was fragmented, linked only by the Church and the Latin tongue. In such a society, the exploration of far-off lands could be supported neither by poverty-stricken kings, nor by merchants whose customers could afford little beyond what was produced in the next town. It is fitting that the farthest-ranging explorations of the time were not inspired by political or commercial purpose, but were accomplished for religious motives: the yearning of Irish monks for deserted islands where they could live in contemplation, far from the temptations of human society.

From Dark Age to Renaissance

By the ninth century, when the Irish had explored and settled oceanic islands at least as far west as Iceland, Europe was beginning to climb out of the "Dark Ages." Kingdoms and empires were growing in size, stability and wealth. Cities and churches of stone were once again being built, but the amount of wealth and trade was still not sufficient to finance oceanic exploration. In the following centuries, exploration of the North Atlantic and the discovery of North America was the by-product of a very different force: the last major outbreak of barbarian peoples across Europe. The eruption of Scandinavian peoples during the ninth and tenth centuries has been explained as the product of climatic change, economic forces in their homelands, the development of maritime skills and technology, or as the simple reactions of poor but hardy marginal peoples to increasingly wealthy and indolent neighbors. Whatever the motive, the forces that overthrew the established kingdoms of Europe also propelled small groups of settlers westward across the North Atlantic, in search of new lands and freedom from royal constraint.

The Norse were the first Europeans to attempt an occupation of what is now Canada, but it was doomed to failure because of the aboriginal peoples' ability to protect their homelands. Nevertheless, the Norse managed to maintain settlements in nearby Greenland for almost five centuries, from which at least occasional voyages continued to be made to the eastern coasts of Canada. Contact was also maintained between Greenland and Europe throughout this period, providing a conduit through which knowledge of Western Atlantic lands could reach the Old World. The extent of such knowledge is suggested by the description, written by an eleventh-century Arab geographer, of a people who are probably Inuit. It may also be shown in the much-discussed "Vinland Map," which displays representations of Greenland and eastern Canada, and which may date from the early fifteenth century.

Consciousness of land in the far northwest may have incited fifteenth-century Portuguese exploration from the Azores, and English exploration to the west of Ireland. The discoveries of these early explorers are only hinted at in maps and accounts of the period, yet these hints suggest that Newfoundland, and perhaps Greenland, may have been known to Portuguese and English mariners a few decades before the voyages of Columbus and Cabot.

New Spain and the New Found Land

The late fifteenth-century voyages of Columbus in the south, and Cabot in the north, were to set the stage for the gradual development of the Spanish and English civilizations of the Americas. These voyages, and the ones that were to follow through the sixteenth century, came from a Europe far different from the one that produced mediaeval Irish monks or expatriate Norsemen. The Crusades had broadened the horizons of Europe, established markets for foreign goods, and probably had been the

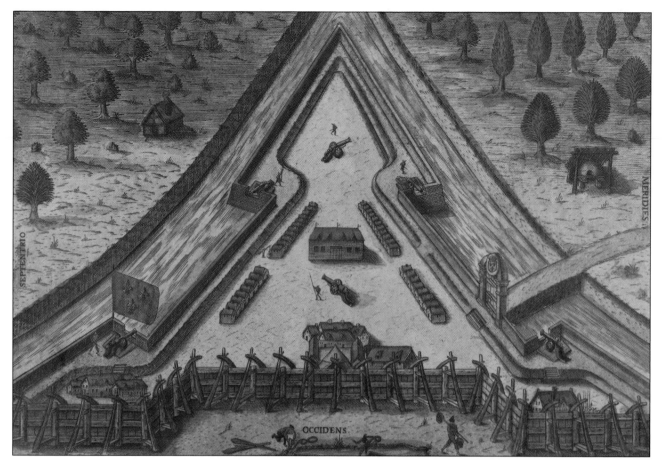

major force in stimulating a revival of trade and commerce throughout the continent. The cities of Italy won the greatest benefits from increased Mediterranean trade. They led Europe in developing both the skills necessary to undertake maritime trade, and the banking and insurance systems which could efficiently finance such endeavours. It is no coincidence that both Columbus and Cabot were Italian, as was Verrazzano, the first official explorer sent to the New World by the king of France.

By the early sixteenth century, Europe had developed the technology, skill and wealth to mount a concerted effort to develop the commercial potential of the newly discovered lands in the west. For the century following the initial voyages, these efforts were directed to two major nodes of New World exploitation. In the south, the Spanish laid claim to New Spain, where they immediately began to subjugate local populations, and to establish Spanish settlements based on the exploitation of Indian labour in mines and on large agricultural estates. Far to the north, in the vicinity of Labrador, Newfoundland and Nova Scotia, lay the territory known as "Baccalaos" or the "New Found Land." Here the Portuguese, Basques,

All early European attempts to settle North America came to bloody ends, at the hands of other Europeans if not at those of the First Peoples. In 1564 the French built Fort Caroline, named after King Charles IX, near what is now Jacksonville, Florida. The following year the Spanish took the fort and massacred the occupants. This drawing was made by Jacques Lemoyne de Morgues, one of the few survivors.

French and increasingly the English developed a massive exploitation of the animal resources of the area: primarily cod, but also seabirds and sea mammals, including the large whales preyed upon by Basque hunters. The extent of the enterprise is suggested by one 1578 report of 50 English ships, 100 Spanish, 50 Portuguese, and 150 French fishing vessels, as well as 20 or 30 whaling ships working Newfoundland waters.

Gold and Silver, Codfish and Whale Oil

It has long been recognized that sixteenth-century Spain accumulated massive amounts of capital by systematically plundering its New World colonies of precious metals and other valuable commodities. The amount of wealth created by plundering the animal resources of the New Found Land has been less widely recognized. Yet, although the comparison is difficult to make, some historians have calculated that sixteenth-century Europe gained more wealth from Newfoundland cod and whale oil than from the gold and silver of Mexico and Peru.

There are several reasons why Canada's major contribution to European development at this time is generally ignored or taken for granted. Fish and oil are smelly, unattractive commodities compared with silver and gold; they were procured, transported and largely consumed by the non-aristocratic segments of European society; and fishing is not nearly so spectacular as conquering an alien race. While the Conquest of New Spain has become a dramatic and important event in European and American history, the contemporaneous Plunder of the New Found Land has been largely forgotten.

Differences between the two kinds of resource exploitation also resulted in remarkable differences in the kinds of enterprises and institutions which Europeans established in New Spain and the New Found Land. The small conquering armies of Spain were immediately followed, and in many cases preceded, by European diseases which caused massive mortality among the dense Indian populations of Central and South America. The accumulation of wealth required that the remaining population be put to work under Spanish supervision and for Spanish profit. This required, in turn, widespread Spanish settlement and the rapid establishment of an administrative structure throughout the territories of New Spain, supplemented by large-scale missionary efforts by the Church.

In contrast, the animal wealth of the New Found Land could be procured without subjugating the aboriginal inhabitants, and without establishing European settlement. Profits could be made by fishing the Newfoundland banks, salting the cod in barrels, and sailing home without going ashore. Even the "dry" cod fishery, in which the salted fish were dried on the beach, or the Basque whaling effort, could be pursued by establishing nothing more than small, temporary shore stations.

The few attempts made by sixteenth-century Europe to establish colonies in North America all met with frustration and abandonment at best, or at worst with disaster. The problems seem to have been the same as those encountered by the Norse when they attempted to settle Vinland 500 years before: the colonies were simply too small and too isolated to withstand the effective defence of their land that was mounted by the aboriginal occupants of the area. The First Peoples of eastern Canada were generally eager to trade with Europeans, as they had for generations traded with Indian travellers from distant lands. They became concerned, however, when the Europeans came ashore and, without the permission of the title-holders to local lands, began to construct buildings and indicate that they planned to stay in the country.

The Norse Vinland colony ended in skirmishes with the local people, as did the 1520s Portuguese settlement on Cape Breton Island and Cartier's 1541 settlement near Québec. Frobisher's relations with the Baffin Island Inuit had degenerated into fighting and hostage-taking, even before his 1578 attempt to establish the first English colony in the New World. Fortunately for the Englishmen who were to be left on Baffin Island, the plan was not carried through. The first Virginia colony, established seven years later, was abandoned after it became involved in hostilities with the local Indians; a second settlement, founded in 1587, disappeared without a trace. By 1600, long after the Spanish conquests of Mexico and Peru, no European colonies existed north of Florida.

Canada Colonized

This picture was to change remarkably during the first decades of the seventeenth century, roughly 100 years after European fishermen had begun to exploit the fishing grounds of eastern Canada. Two related developments can be seen as the primary reasons for the establishment of successful colonies at this time. One was the growing importance of the fur trade, which had begun before Cartier's time, and become an increasingly profitable sideline for sixteenth-century European fishermen. By the end of the century, Europe's developing taste for hats manufactured from beaver fur had made trading more profitable than fishing, and shore stations were being established to exploit the trade. Like the gold of New Spain, Canadian beaver fur gave Europeans the wealth and incentive to establish permanent communities ashore, and to develop relationships with the native peoples of the country.

The other development which opened the door to successful colonization was the decimation of local Indian populations by the introduction of European diseases. The Jesuit Father Pierre Biard, reporting on the Micmac and other Indians of Acadia during his stay from 1611 to 1613, stated:

They are astonished and often complain that, since the French mingle with and carry on trade with them, they are dying fast and the population is thinning out. For they assert that, before this association and intercourse, all their countries were very populous and they tell how one by one the different coasts, according as they have begun to traffic with us, have been more reduced by disease...

By the time Biard was writing, introduced diseases to which New World peoples lacked any immunity or tolerance had been sweeping the continent for almost a century. The native populations of Florida and the Caribbean islands were already well on their way to extinction, and the populations of Mexico and Peru had probably been reduced by more than half. Epidemic disease spread more slowly through the sparse populations of more northern regions, but eventually was just as devastating.

In 1603, when Champlain explored the St. Lawrence River, he found the area an uninhabited no-man's-land between the Iroquois to the south and Algonkian groups to the north. The numerous peoples among whom Cartier had travelled in the 1530s — the inhabitants of Stadacona, Hochelaga and other villages — had simply disappeared. Meagre evidence suggests that the sixteenth-century St. Lawrence Iroquois were at war with the Iroquoian peoples to the south of Lake Ontario, or the Hurons to the north of the lake. Perhaps these wars were caused by the lucrative trade with Europeans that was developing along the lower St. Lawrence. But aboriginal warfare rarely entailed massive casualties, or the massacre of women and children. The St. Lawrence Iroquois almost certainly fell victim to European diseases as well, a process that may have started as early as the winter of 1535 when Cartier reported an epidemic in the village of Stadacona.

As a result, the St. Lawrence Valley was uninhabited when Champlain established the first permanent settlement at Québec in 1608. In the following decades, the French were able to expand and consolidate their occupation of an area where there were no living aboriginal owners. The Pilgrims who landed at Plymouth Rock in 1620 also encountered a dying local population. One immigrant reported that:

...the bones and skulls upon the severall places of their habitations made such a spectacle after my coming into those partes, that, as I travailed in the Forrest nere the Massachusetts, it seemed to me a new found Golgotha.

The Pilgrims thanked God for having swept the land clean of heathens, so that it could be put to use for the support of Christian people. The first governor of the Massachusetts colony wrote: "For the natives, they are neere all dead of small Poxe, so as the Lord hathe cleared our title to what we possess."

The decimation or disappearance of eastern seaboard populations during the first century of contact with Europeans must have been the major factor in opening North America to European settlement. Successful and long-lasting colonies were established in 1605 at Port Royal in what is now Nova Scotia; in 1607 at Jamestown, Virginia; in 1608 at Québec; 1610 at Cupids and 1621 at Ferryland, both on Newfoundland's Avalon Peninsula; 1615 at Manhattan Island; 1620 at Plymouth, Massachusetts; and at numerous other localities over the next few decades. After five centuries of unsuccessful attempts at settlement, Europeans were suddenly capable of establishing beach-heads of occupation in North America. The European conquest of the New World had truly begun.

ACKNOWLEDGEMENTS

This book owes a great debt to the many colleagues with whom I have discussed the fascinating questions relating to early European visits to the New World. I wish especially to thank Jim Tuck, who introduced me to the wonderful archaeology of initial European settlement in Newfoundland and Labrador. My work on the mediaeval Norse in Arctic Canada has been greatly aided by discussions with Gwyn Jones, Tom McGovern, Peter Schledermann and Birgitta Wallace among others. As usual, my greatest debt is to Patricia Sutherland for her interest, ideas and encouragement.

INDEX

Acadia, 170
Acadie, 110
Admiral of the Ocean Sea, 82 (see Columbus)
Aegean Sea, 19
Africa (Central), 13
Africa (North), 24, 30, 41, 109, 112
Africa (West), 21, 158
Alaska, 15, 16, 52, 147
Alberta, 15
Alexander the Great, 78, 152
Alfonse, Jean, 134, 135
Alfred the Great, 24
Algonkians, 15, 170
Al-Idrisi, 54
Alvarez, John, 101 (see also Fagundes, Joam Alvarez)
Ameralik Fjord, 60
Americans, 147
Andreason, Claus, 59
Angoulême, 109 (see also New York)
Anticosti Island, 120, 128
Antilia, 65, 76, 79, 95, 97
Antwerp, 87, 151
Aquila, 137
Arabian Sea, 20
Arabic, 74, 88, 112, 167
Arcadia, 110
Arctic Ocean, 14
Arctic, 14, 16, 30, 33, 49, 52, 53, 54, 56, 57, 142, 146, 147, 158, 160, 162, 164, 166
Ardagh, 23
Armada, 75, 153
Asia (Central), 13
Asia (Eastern), 112
Asia (Southeast), 13
Athabaskans (language), 15 (see Dene)
Atlantic Ocean, 8, 9, 11, 17, 18, 20, 21, 22, 23, 24, 26, 27, 29, 30, 31, 32, 42, 43, 44, 46, 50, 54, 57, 58, 59, 62, 66, 68, 70, 71, 72, 73, 74, 75, 76, 78, 79, 81, 82, 83, 84, 88, 90, 94, 95, 96, 97, 101, 104, 105, 108, 110, 111, 128, 147, 150, 158, 160, 161, 164, 167
Atlantic Provinces, 16 (see Maritime Provinces)
Atlantis, 72, 78
Aubert, Thomas, 102
Australia, 18
Avalon (Land of), 72
Avalon Peninsula, 170
Avon River, 19
Ayde, 164
Azoreans, 58, 94, 99, 100
Azores, 20, 30, 58, 74, 76, 79, 94, 95, 97, 98, 99, 146, 167

Aztecs 14
164, 165, 166, 167, 168, 169

Baccalaos, 8, 94, 109, 168 (see also Newfoundland)
Baccalieu Island, 162
Bacon, Robert, 84
Baffin Bay, 29, 30, 165
Baffin Island, 44, 46, 51, 57, 58, 62, 68, 69, 156, 160, 163, 165, 166, 169
Baghdad, 41
Baia da Espera, 162 (see Bay d'Espoir)
Baia de Cocepicion (see Conception Bay)
Baltimore (Lord), 8 (see Calver, Sir George)
Baltic Sea, 43
Bardarson, Ivar, 160
Barents Sea, 30
Barkham, Selma, 143, 144, 149
Basel Council, 64
Basque, 102, 144, 147, 148, 153, 168
Bauld, Cape, 91
Bay Despair, 162 (see Bay d'Espoir)
Bay d'Espoir, 162
Beardmore, 38, 40
Beare, James, 156
Beauvais, Vincent de, 64
Beheim, Martin, 65
Belem Tower, 94
Belle Isle (Strait of), 47, 92, 100, 115, 116, 117, 120, 122, 129, 138, 141, 142, 143, 144, 152, 153, 162, 163
Benincasa, Grazioso, 76
Beothuk, 16, 101, 102
Bering Land Bridge, 10
Bering Strait, 16
Bermuda, 76
Best, George, 156, 165
Biard, Pierre, 170
Biscaye (Bay of), 69, 147
Bjorn, 35
Black Sea, 44
Blanc (Cape), 118 (see Percé, Cape)
Blanc-Sablon, 117, 120, 122, 128, 162
Blasket Islands, 76
Blessed Isles, 8, 72
Bonavista Bay, 79
Bonavista (Cape), 116, 162
Bordeaux, 91
Brador Bay, 117
Brador Lake, 101
Brasil Island, 62, 76, 79, 82, 83,

88, 90, 94, 95, 97
Brasyle, Island of (see Brasil, Island)
Brazil, 98, 99, 113, 116
Brazil Rocks, 79
Bremen, 73
Brendan, 26, 27
Brendan (St.), 23, 26, 27, 32, 33, 34, 78, 152
Brest, 117 (see Vieux Fort Bay)
Britain, 19, 20, 29, 32, 108
Brittany, 26, 29, 90, 108, 109, 115
Bretons, 26, 86, 108, 109, 113
Bristol, 81, 82, 83, 84, 88, 90, 92, 94, 99, 100, 160, 165
Bristol Channel, 18
British Columbia, 9, 14
British Isles, 30, 32, 33, 44, 46, 95, 109, 159
British Museum, 65
Britons, 14, 109
Buttus, 144, 149

Cabo da Espera, 162 (see Spear, Cape)
Cabo de Bohaventura, 162 (see Bonavista, Cape)
Cabo de Prado, 118 (see Pré, Cap du)
Cabo dos Bretones, 162 (see Cape Breton Island)
Cabo Raso, 162 (see Race, Cape)
Cabot Strait, 102, 118, 138
Cabot, John, 7, 8, 60, 62, 69, 70, 74, 75, 76, 78, 79, 81, 82, 83, 84, 86, 87, 88, 89, 90, 91, 92, 94, 96, 98, 99, 100, 101, 108, 109, 110, 121, 142, 151, 161, 162, 167, 168
Cabot, Sebastian, 82, 115, 159
Caboto, Giovanni, 88 (see Cabot, John)
Caesar, Julius, 26
Cain's Land, 107, 117, 128
California, University of, 67
Calver, Sir George (see Lord Baltimore)
Canada, 123, 124, 125, 126, 128, 139 (see Stadacona)
Canadian Museum of Civilization, 105
Canaries Islands, 20, 21, 72, 76, 79, 84, 94
Canso (Strait of), 106
Cantino, Alberto, 69, 99
Cape Breton Island, 7, 90, 91, 101, 102, 106, 109, 115, 121, 133, 162, 163, 169

Cape of the Bretons, 162 (see Cape Breton Island)
Cape Verde, 20
Cap Rouge, 121, 137, 138, 139
Cape Verde Islands, 79, 94, 98
Cape York District, 59
Caraquet, 137
Caribbean, 7, 16, 30, 50, 74, 76, 82, 87, 91, 98, 109, 113, 130, 160, 170
Caroline (Fort), 168
Carolina (North), 110
Carolinas, 110, 162
Carpini, Giovanni, 112
Carthage, 19, 20
Carthaginians, 19
Cartier, Jacques, 7, 8, 11, 15, 60, 106, 107, 108, 109, 111, 115, 116, 117, 118, 120, 121, 122, 123, 124, 125, 126, 128, 129, 130, 131, 132, 133, 135, 136, 137, 138, 139, 142, 161, 162, 165, 169, 170
Caspian Mountains, 112
Cathay, 65, 88, 92, 156 (see China)
Caverio, Nicolo, 67, 69
Chaleurs Bay, 108, 118
Champlain, Samuel, 8, 10, 11, 105, 170
Charlemagne, 29
Charles VIII of France, 137
Charles IX of France, 168
Charlesbourg Royal, 136, 137, 138, 139
Chasteaux (Hable des), 116, 162 (see Chateau Bay)
Chasteaux (Baie des), 143 (see Chateau Bay)
Chateau Bay, 117, 143, 162
Chicago Tribune, 62
Chicago, 65, 67
China, 13, 65, 78, 88, 92, 96, 110, 112, 113, 156
China (Northern), 112
Chinese, 105
Cipangu, 65, 76, 112 (see Japan)
Cobalt, 164
Cod (Cape), 111
Colomba (St), 29
Colombus, Christopher, 7, 8, 17, 38, 48, 58, 62, 63, 64, 65, 70, 74, 75, 76, 79, 81, 82, 83, 84, 88, 89, 91, 94, 100, 113, 130, 150, 161, 167, 168
Company of Cathay, 164
Conception Bay, 162
Confederation (Canadian), 90
Constantinople, 41, 44
Corea, 72

Corte-Real, Gaspar, 58, 59, 60, 62, 66, 69, 100, 102, 106, 109, 129
Corte-Real, Joao Vaz, 58, 97, 98, 106
Corte-Real, Miguel, 58, 67, 70, 100, 101, 106
Corte-Real, Vasqueanes, 58, 106
Cortes, Hernan, 108, 126, 130
Corvo Island, 20, 79, 94
Cosa, Juan de la, 89
Countess of Warwick Island, 164, 165
Countess of Warwick Sound, 163
Cree (language), 15
Cromer, 84
Crusades, 72, 74, 96, 112, 150, 167
Cuba, 76
Cupids, 170

Damoiselle (Île de la), 134, 135 (see Harrington Islands)
Denmark, 43, 84
Danish, 41, 58, 59
Dartford, 165
Dauphine, 110
Davis Strait, 57, 58
Day, John, 82, 90, 91, 92
Dead Sea, 67
Dene, 15
Denys, Jean, 115
Desceliers, Pierre, 133, 153
Devon Island, 53
Dicuil, 29, 32, 33
Dieppe, 102, 125
Dingle Peninsula, 29
Disko Bay, 52, 57
Domagaya, 128, 132
Donnacona, 118, 120, 128, 129, 132, 133, 136
Dublin, 34
Dursey Head, 91, 92

East St. Modeste, 144
Egede, Niels, 59
Egypt, 13, 72
Egyptians, 19
Einarsson, Bjorn, 53
El Dorado, 132
Elizabeth I, 156, 158, 161, 164
Ellesmere Island, 52, 53, 56
Elyot, Hugh, 83
England, 18, 24, 32, 44, 74, 75, 78, 81, 82, 84, 86, 89, 90, 96, 100, 110, 121, 153, 155, 156, 164, 165, 166, 169
English, 58, 59, 76, 79, 82, 83, 84, 86, 89, 94, 99, 108, 109, 110, 147, 160
English Channel, 18
Engroneland Island, 78
Eirik the Red, 34, 38, 44, 52, 54, 150, 162
Eriksson, Leif, 45, 48, 49, 54, 68
Eriksson, Thorsttein, 46, 49
Eriksson, Thorvald, 46, 48, 49, 50

Eskimo, 147
Estotiland Island, 78
Europe (Northern), 44, 54, 73, 109
Europe (Southern), 70

Faereyjar, 32 (see Faeroe Islands)
Faeroe Islands, 27, 32, 33, 44, 105
Fagundes, Joam Alvarez, 101, 102, 118, 120
Farewell (Cape), 67, 68, 105
Fear (Cape), 110
Fernandez, Joao, 98, 99, 100, 118
Ferryland, 170
Fixlandia, 95 (see Iceland)
Florence, 150, 151
Flores Island, 79, 94
Florida, 46, 109, 110, 113, 115, 118, 168, 169, 170
Fogo Island, 162
Formigas Rocks, 79
France, 7, 11, 30, 108, 110, 113, 115, 117, 120, 121, 122, 123, 124, 126, 128, 132, 133, 134, 135, 136, 137, 138, 139, 163, 168, 169
France-Roy, 138, 139
François I, 108, 110, 116, 134
French, 102, 107, 108, 109, 120, 125, 126, 129, 130, 131, 132, 135, 135, 138, 139, 160, 168, 170,
Frisland Island, 78
Frobisher Bay, 163, 165, 166
Frobisher Strait, 156, 161
Frobisher, Martin, 8, 75, 78, 155, 158, 159, 160, 161, 163, 164, 165, 166, 169
Frobisher's Streytes, 163 (see Frobisher Strait)
Fundy Bay, 110, 111
Funk Islands, 116, 128

Gabriel, 75, 161, 163
Gallarus, 29
Gaspé, 13, 111, 118, 121, 124, 128
Gastaldi, 109
Gauls, 14
Genoa, 88
George, 83
Germans, 58, 59, 84
Germany (Northern), 84
Germany, 64, 65, 73
Ghana, 158
Gibraltar (Strait of), 19, 20
Gilbert, Sir Humphrey, 158, 159, 165
Gironde, 91
Glace Bay, 106
Glaumbauer, 148
Glendalough, 29
Gnupsson, Eirik, 68
Gog (Tribe), 112
Gomez, 117, 118, 120
Göteborg, 21
Grace Dieu, 74
Grand Banks, 30, 86, 92, 106

Grand Bay, 75, 122, 143, 148, 152, 153 (see Belle Isle, Strait of)
Grande Hermine, 128
Great Lakes, 16, 46, 142
Greece, 14, 110
Greek, 72
Grenier, Robert, 149
Greenland, 8, 29, 30, 34, 35, 41, 43, 44, 46, 47, 48, 49, 50, 51, 52, 54, 56, 57, 58, 59, 60, 61, 62, 64, 66, 67, 68, 69, 70, 72, 78, 88, 93, 95, 97, 98, 99, 100, 104, 105, 110, 115, 142, 147, 158, 159, 160, 161, 162, 164, 165, 167
Greenland Museum, 59
Greenlanders, 8, 49, 50, 53
Greenwich, 161
Griquet, 92
Gronelada, 62 (see Greenland)
Guanches, 76
Guatemala, 13
Gulf Stream, 29, 30, 94
Gunnalangson, Gudleif, 35

Hakluyt, Richard, 136
Hall, Charles Francis, 166
Hanno, 19
Harald Haarfager, 44
Harrington Islands, 134
Hatteras (Cape), 110
Hebrides Islands, 27, 29
Helluland, 46, 51, 57, 68, 69, 72
Henricus, 68 (see Gnupsson)
Henry the Navigator, 74, 76, 79
Henri II of France, 133
Henry VII of England, 82, 89, 90, 99, 100
Henry VIII of England, 158
Herjolfsness, 53
Herjulfsson, Bjarni, 46, 88
Hern Island, 105
Herodotus, 19
Hesiod, 72
Hibernia, 29 (see also Ireland)
Hochelaga, 11, 124, 125, 126, 128, 129, 130, 131, 132, 137, 139, 170 (see Tutonaguy)
Hochelagans, 125, 130
Holy City, 112 (see Jerusalem)
Holy Land, 112, 150
Homo sapiens, 10, 18
Honfleur, 115
Honguedo, 128 (see Gaspé)
Hormuz, 113
Hrafn the Limerick-Farer, 34
Huang-Ho (Valley of), 10
Hudson Strait, 58, 68, 100, 159, 165
Hungary, 112
Huron, 10, 170
Huron (Lake), 16
Hvalsey, 52
Hvitramannaland, 34, 35
Hy-Brasil, 76 (see Brasil Island)

Icaria Island, 78
Ice Age, 18
Ilha de Pitiguoem, 101 (see

Penguin Island)
Illa Verde, 95, 97, 100
Incas, 13, 20, 88, 112
Indians, 7, 9, 13, 14, 15, 16, 46, 47, 49, 50, 60, 100, 101, 102, 106, 110, 117, 118, 120, 121, 122, 124, 126, 129, 130, 131, 132, 133, 135, 136, 137, 138, 139, 142, 153, 160, 169, 170
Indies, 65, 123
Indus (Valley of), 10
Ingjaldur, 60
Ingjali, 60 (see Ingjaldur)
Ingjoldsholl, 88
Ingonish, 106
Ingstad, Helge, 46, 47
Innocent IV, 96
Insulae Fortunatae, 72, 76, 79
Inuit, 16, 34, 51, 52, 53, 54, 56, 57, 59, 60, 61, 68, 146, 147, 153, 159, 160, 163, 164, 165, 166, 167, 169
Iona, 29, 44
Irish, 23, 26, 27, 29, 33, 34, 42, 46, 72, 73, 76, 78, 104, 150, 167
Irishman Islands, 34
Ireland, 18, 23, 24, 26, 27, 29, 32, 33, 34, 69, 70, 76, 83, 88, 90, 91, 92, 94, 95, 100, 167
Iroquoians, 11, 16, 120, 125, 126, 170
Iroquois, 15, 120, 123, 125, 130, 132, 136, 137, 139, 170
Iscariot, Judas, 26
Islam, 112
Iceland, 8, 16, 20, 21, 23, 27, 29, 30, 32, 33, 34, 35, 39, 41, 43, 44, 46, 47, 48, 49, 50, 53, 56, 58, 60, 70, 72, 73, 83, 84, 88, 90, 95, 97, 104, 105, 108, 152, 162, 167
Icelanders, 69, 84, 88, 90
Islettes (les), 117 (see Brador Bay)
Islond, William, 90
Israelites, 78
Italian, 76, 78, 105, 110, 150
Italy, 10, 108, 112, 137, 150, 168

Jacksonville, 168
Jacques Cartier Bay, 117
Jacques Cartier Bridge, 130
Jamestown, 170
Japan, 65, 76, 112
Jasconius, 34
Jerusalem, 112
Jerusalem Farer, 53 (see Einarsson, Bjorn)

Kangek, Aaron of, 57
Karakorum, 96
Karlsefni, Snorri, 46, 49
Kalsefni, Thorfinn, 46, 48, 49
Karpont (hable de), 116, 162 (see Quirpon)
Kensington Stone, 39
Kenyon, Walter, 166
Kodlunarn Island, 161, 163, 164, 165, 166

Kolnus, Jan, 58 (see Scolvus, Johannes)
Kublai Khan, 96
Kuyuk, 96

Labrador, 15, 29, 30, 34, 35, 44, 46, 49, 57, 58, 66, 68, 69, 70, 90, 93, 97, 98, 100, 117, 121, 128, 141, 147, 149, 152, 153, 159, 160, 163, 168 (see also Markland)
Labrador Current, 29, 30, 142
Labrador Sea, 30, 160
Lachine Rapids, 137, 139
Lahontan (Baron de), 15
Land of Cortereal, 109
Land of the Bretons, 109, 139 (see Cape Breton Island)
Land of the Promise of the Saints, 26, 72, 76
Land of Evil People, 11
Land of the Labrador, 99, 100, 101, 110
Land of the King of Portugal, 70, 101
Land's End (Cape), 19
L'Anse-Amour, 142
L'Anse-aux-Meadows, 44, 46, 47, 48, 49, 50, 69, 92
La Rochelle, 109, 111, 117
Las Casas, Bartolome de, 94, 97
Lebanon, 19
Lemoyne de Morgues, Jacques, 168
Leon, Ponce de, 110
Le Testu, Guillaume, 129
Lewis, Harrison F., 121
Limerick, 35
Limoëlou, 138
Lindisfarne, 44
Lisbon, 94, 100
Lloyd, John, 58 (see Scolvus, Johannes)
Loks Land, 163, 164
London, 83, 90, 161
Louisbourg, 106
Lyons, 110, 150

Macdonald Stewart Foundation, 138
Machu Picchu, 16
Magdalen Islands, 118, 124, 132, 133
Madeira, 20, 76, 79, 94, 110
Madoc, 78
Madrid, 114
Magellan, F., 113
Magellan (Strait of), 109, 113, 158, 163
Magog (Tribe), 112
Maine, 39, 49, 91, 110
Malecite, 16
Manhattan Island, 170
Manuel I, 98
Mar del Sur, 158 (see Pacific Ocean)
Maritime Provinces, 13, 16, 110
Markland, 46, 49, 50, 57, 68, 69, 72, 88 (see also Labrador)

Marseille, 20
Massachusetts, 7, 170
Massalia, 20 (see Marseille)
Massard, Léopold, 138
Masson, Ari, 34
Mathew, 75, 90
Mayda Island, 95
Mayflower, 170
McGill University, 124
Mecca, 88
Moors, 100
Medici (Bank), 151
Mediterranean, 27, 72, 74, 76, 88, 168
Melville Bay, 67, 68, 69
Memorial University, 144
Mercator, 78
Mesopotamia, 10
Meta Incognita, 8, 155, 156, 164, 165, 166
Mexico Valley, 14, 50
Mexico City, 131
Mexico, 7, 8, 10, 11, 13, 14, 108, 109, 114, 125, 130, 139, 169, 170
Mexico (Gulf of), 16
Michael, 161
Micmac, 13, 16, 102, 106, 118, 120, 170
Milan Chart, 95, 97, 100
Ming 112
Minnesota, 39, 50
Mira Bay, 106
Mississipi, 50
Mississipi Valley, 46
Missouri Valley, 15
Molinus, 117
Mongol, 62, 96
Mongol Empire, 76
Mont St. Michel Abbey, 116
Montagnais, 16
Montecalunya, Juan Caboto, 88
Montréal Island, 129, 130, 132, 137
Montréal (City of), 125, 130, 138, 139
Morgan, Louis Henry, 130
Morison, Samuel Eliot, 35, 92
Mount Royal, 129, 130, 132
Mowat, Farley, 43
Muscovy Company, 161

Nabaitsoq, 60 (see Nipaitsoq)
Narragansett Bay, 109, 110
Nass River, 9
Natashquan, 120
Navaranak, 59
Navarre, Marguerite de, 134
Necho II, 19
Nepean (Point), 105
Netherlands, 73
New Found Island, 8
New Found Land, 81, 82, 86, 99, 100, 168
Newfoundland, 8, 16, 26, 27, 29, 30, 44, 46, 58, 59, 62, 66, 69, 70, 75, 76, 79, 86, 87, 88, 90, 91, 92, 94, 97, 98, 99, 100, 101, 102, 106, 108, 109, 110, 11, 113, 114, 115, 116, 117, 118, 122, 132, 133, 136, 138,

139, 144, 151, 153, 159, 160, 162, 163, 167, 168, 169, 170 (see also Vinland)
Newfoundland Banks, 160, 169 (see Grand Banks)
Newfoundlanders, 90
New Brunswick, 118, 137
New England, 90, 162
New France, 15, 109
New Jersey, 110
New Spain, 7, 75, 109, 110, 114, 126, 130, 151, 167, 168, 169, 170
New York City, 109
New York (Bay of), 110
New York State, 125, 126
Nile River, 19
Nile Valley, 10
Nina, 75, 84
Nipaitsoq, 59, 60
Noël, Jacques, 139
North Sea, 18, 43
Nordrsetur, 56
Northwest Passage, 155, 156, 158, 159, 160, 164, 165
Norumbega, 111, 113
Norman, 54, 86, 108
Norse, 16, 30, 32, 33, 34, 35, 37, 38, 39, 41, 42, 43, 44, 46, 47, 48, 49, 50, 51, 52, 53, 54, 56, 57, 58, 59, 60, 61, 64, 67, 68, 70, 72, 73, 76, 78, 88, 90, 92, 104, 106, 150, 160, 167, 169 (see also Viking)
Norway, 20, 30, 33, 38, 43, 44, 62, 64, 104, 105
Norwegian, 41, 54
Nova Scotia, 79, 86, 93, 97, 101, 102, 109, 110, 111, 121, 162, 168, 170

Ochelassa, 129 (see Hochelaga)
Ohio River, 50
Ohio Valley, 14
Oklahoma, 39
Olaf Kyrre, 49
Ontario, 16, 17, 38, 125, 164
Ontario (Lake), 170
Orkneys, 26, 27, 29, 44, 78
Orléans (île d'), 128, 129
Osiris, 72
Ottawa City, 105
Ottawa River, 130, 132
Ottawa Valley, 105
Ottoman Empire, 112
Ouaiseaux (île des), 116 (see Funk Islands)

Pacific Ocean, 14, 96, 147, 158, 163
Paleoeskimos, 49, 142
Pamlico Sound, 110
Papars, 33
Paraguay, 39
Parks Canada, 47, 149
Paris, 95, 97, 126
Pasqualigo, Pietro, 100, 101
Patrick (St.), 24
Penguin Islands, 102
Percé (Cape), 118

Peru, 7, 8, 10, 14, 16, 139, 169, 170
Persian Gulf, 113
Petite Hermine, 121, 128
Phoenicians, 19, 20, 100
Philip II, 148
Pilgrims, 7, 170
Pillars of Hercules, (see Gibraltar, Strait of)
Pining, Diddrik, 58, 84
Pinware River, 144
Pissaro, 126
Plains, 14, 15
Platon, 72
Plymouth, 170
Plymouth Rock, 7, 170
Polo, 76
Polo, Marco, 76, 96, 112, 113
Polo, Matteo, 76, 96, 113
Polo, Niccolo, 76, 96, 113
Poland, 72, 96, 112
Port du Refuge, 109 (see Narragansett Bay)
Port Royal, 170
Portugal, 30, 58, 74, 76, 79, 83, 94, 97, 98, 99, 100, 101, 102, 106, 108, 129, 158
Portuguese, 20, 58, 59, 70, 74, 76, 79, 93, 94, 97, 98, 99, 100, 101, 102, 106, 108, 110, 113, 160. 167. 168
Pothorst, 58
Prado (Cabo de), 118 (see Percé, Cape)
Pré (Cap du), 118
Prester John (Land of), 72, 112
Prince Edward Island, 118
Public Archives of Canada, 143
Pytheas, 20

Qilakitsoq, 56
Québec City, 8, 16, 120, 121, 125, 128, 169, 170
Québec Province, 49, 106, 117, 125, 128
Queen Elizabeth Foreland, 161 (see Resolution Island)
Quinn, David, 82, 83, 88, 91, 92
Quirpon, 116, 136, 162

Race (Cape), 91, 133, 162
Rafn, Carl Christian, 38, 41
Raleigh, Sir Walter, 8, 106
Ramah Bay, 49
Ramusio, 86, 131
Red Bay, 141, 143, 144, 147, 148, 149, 152, 166
Renaissance, 92, 131, 156, 167
Renews, 133
Resolution Island, 161
Restelo, 94
Rhode Island, 38, 39, 50, 110
Rink, Hinrich, 59, 60
Roberval, 121, 129, 133, 134, 135, 136, 138, 139
Roche, Marguerite de la, 134, 135, 139
Rocky Bay, 121
Rocky Mountains, 14

Roman Empire, 24, 167
Romans, 14, 20, 76
Rome, 14, 21
Roskilde Fjord, 43
Rougnouse, 133 (see Renews)
Royal Ontario Museum, 38, 40, 166
Rubruck, Wilhelm, 112
Russia, 41, 44
Rut, John, 160

Sable Island, 102
Sabo, Deborah, 56
Saddle Island, 141, 144, 149, 152, 153
Sagnay, 133 (see Saguenay, Kingdom of)
Saguenay (Kingdom of), 8, 124, 128, 130, 132, 133, 136, 137, 138, 139
Saguenay River, 128
Saguené (rivière de), 129 (see Saguenay River)
Sainct Laurens (baye), 128 (see St Lawrence, Gulf and River)
Saint Marie rapids, 137
St. Brendan's Isle, 62, 76, 78, 79
St. Charles River, 121, 128
St. John's day, 90
St. John's (City), 59, 106, 138, 162
St. Lawrence (lower), 170
St. Lawrence River, 118, 120, 128, 129, 130, 131, 132, 133, 139, 170
St. Lawrence (Gulf of), 8, 16, 69, 102, 111, 113, 116, 117, 118, 120, 121, 122, 124, 134, 135, 137, 142, 144, 153, 162, 163
St. Lawrence Valley, 16, 50, 120, 124, 125, 170
St. Lawrence (Upper), 16, 130
St. Malo, 116, 117, 120, 1212, 122, 124, 126, 132, 133, 136, 138
St. Modeste, 143 (see East St. Modeste)
St. Pierre (Lake), 129
St. Servan, 121 (see Rocky Bay)
Salisbury, 19
San juan, 149, 152
Santa Clara ,84 (see Nina)
Santa Maria, 89
Sargasso Sea, 30, 31
Scandinavia, 21, 39, 41, 160
Schledermann, Peter, 53
Schonback, Bengt, 47
Scolp, Jon, 58 (see Scolvus, Johannes)
Scolvsen, Jon, 58 (see Scolvus Johannes)
Scolvus, Johannes, 58
Scotia, 32 (see also Ireland)
Scotland, 26, 27, 32
Scottish, 78, 147
Semadet, 143 (see East St. Modeste)
Senegal, 79

Seven Cities (Island of), 76, 79, 83, 91, 95, 97
Sept-Iles, 129
Severin, Timothy, 26, 27
Shakespeare, 156
Shetland Islands, 26, 27, 29, 32, 44, 72, 105, 161
Siberia, 16, 49
Sicily, 54
Siena, 151
Simancas, 82
Sinclair, Prince Henry, 78
Skraelings, 50, 52, 53, 54, 57, 59
Snaefellsnes, 88
Soolacadie, 106 (see Mira Bay)
Southampton, 74
Spain, 14, 75, 78, 82, 83, 88, 97, 98, 112, 113, 118, 143, 148, 152, 153, 158, 169
Spanish, 30, 98, 110, 113, 158, 160, 167, 168
Spear (Cape), 162
Speculum Historiale, 64
Spitsbergen, 30, 147
Stadacona, 121, 128, 129, 130, 132, 133, 136, 170 (see Québec City)
Stadaconans, 121, 128, 129, 132, 136
Stefansson, Sigurdur, 46, 69
Stefansson, Vilhjalmur, 160
Stine, Anne, 47
Stonehenge, 18, 19
Strait of the Three Brothers, 58
Straumfjord, 142
Switzerland, 64
Superior (Lake), 40
Sutherland, Patricia, 56
Sweden, 21
Syria, 112

Tagus, 100
Taignoagny, 128, 132
Tamerlane, 112
Tartar Relation, 62, 64
Tartary, 94
Teotihuacan, 14
Terceira, 98, 100
Terra Cortereal, 69, 101
Terra Corte Regalis, 106
Tera del Rey de Portuguall, 69, 99, 101
Terra do Laurador, 101
Terra Laboratoris, 99
Terra Verde, 100, 102
Thames River, 165
Thévet, André, 109, 111, 134, 135
Thiennot, 120, 122
Thor, 33
Thorne, Robert, 83
Thule, 20
Tierra del Fuego, 162
Tieve, Diogo de, 94
Tikal, 13
Tipperary County, 24
Tir Breasail, 76 (see Land of the Promise of the Saints)
Toledo, 148
Toltecs, 14

Tordesillas (treaty), 97, 98, 99, 101
Toronto, 40, 166
Toscanelli, Paolo, 76
Trade Winds, 30
Trigger, Bruce, 124
Trinity, 83
Tuck, James, 144, 148, 149, 152, 153
Tudor, 78
Tunis, 79
Turkey, 113
Turks, 112,113
Tutonaguy, 126, 130, 137 (see Montréal, City)

Ulster, 24
Ultima Thule, 20
Ungava, 49
Ungortok, 59, 60
United States, 7, 14, 16, 50, 62, 69, 105, 110, 125
Unknown Land, 164 (see Meta Incognita)
Upernavik, 67
Upper Rhineland, 64

Valencia, 88
Vatican, 98
Velasco, Pedro de, 94
Velho, Gonçalo, 79
Venice, 74, 76, 78, 88, 101
Verrazano, Giovanni da, 107, 108, 111, 113, 116, 118, 150, 162, 168
Verrazano Narrows, 110
Vestmannaeyar, 34 (see also Irishman Islands)
Vestmenn, 33 (see also Irish)
Vianna, 101, 102
Vieux-Fort Bay, 117
Viking, 20, 23, 29, 37, 38, 39, 41, 44, 50, 73, 150 (see also Norse)
Vinland, 8, 34, 37, 46, 47, 48, 54, 62, 63, 64, 65, 66, 67, 68, 69, 70, 72, 88, 92, 106, 142, 167, 169
Vinland Island, 64, 68, 69
Virgil, Polydore, 90
Vistula River, 96

Wales, 18, 19, 26, 78
Wallace, Birgitta, 47
Welsh, 78
Weser, 73
Westerlies, 30
West England, 165 (see Groenland)
West Indies, 79, 89 (see also Antilles)
White Fleet, 106
White Men's Island, 163 (see Kodlunarn Island)
Wicklow County, 29
World War I, 147
Worcestre, William, 76, 84

Xateau, 143 see Chateau Bay
Xoracadie, 106 (see Mira Bay)

Yahgan, 162
Yale University, 62, 64, 65, 66
Ylha do Fogo, 162 (see Fogo Island)
Ylha dos Bacalhaos, 162 (see Baccalieu Island)
Yslond, William, 90

Zeno, Antonio, 78
Zeno, Nicolo, 78
Zichmni (Prince), 78

ROBERT McGHEE, author of *Canada Rediscovered* and of *Ancient Canada*, was born in Wiarton, Ontario. He studied archaeology at the University of Toronto and the University of Calgary. Since 1965, he has been working on archaeological excavations in the far north, from Labrador to the Mackenzie Delta. This activity has led to a particular interest in Inuit history and in the development of their culture and their way of life. The author of numerous books and articles, he is head of the scientific section of the Archaeological Survey of Canada at the Canadian Museum of Civilization. *Canada Rediscovered* is Professor McGhee's thirteenth book.

GILLES ARCHAMBAULT prepared thirty-one original paintings to illustrate *Ancient Canada*, and eighteen paintings and illustrations for the second volume of the collection. He worked as an illustrator and photographer before turning full-time to his greatest passion, painting. His work is a hymn of praise to the rural landscapes of Québec. Mr. Archambault's special talent for presenting simple scenes of daily life has gained him exibitions in Montreal, Ottawa, Toronto and Boston. A number of his works are housed in private collections in Canada, the U.S., France and Saudi Arabia.

FRANCIS BACK honed his skills as an illustrator at the École des Beaux-Arts in Basel, Switzerland. A specialist in the depiction of historical subjects, he has produced tableaux and frescoes for the Canadian Museum of Civilization and the fortress at Louisbourg; illustrated books that have been published in Canada, the U.S., and England; and designed costumes and sets for historical films. He has also prepared almost two hundred illustrations for National Film Board productions dealing with everyday life in New France. Fascinated by the history of costume, he has been carrying out exhaustive archival research on the subject for the past ten years. He has written and illustrated numerous articles on the origins of Amerindian and Canadian costumes. The artist is inspired by a twofold challenge: to make history live while at the same time rigorously respecting documentary sources.

CLAUDE PAULETTE began his career as a journalist at Radio-Canada. Then, won over to publishing, he edited the magazine *Culture vivante*, published by Quebec's Ministère des Affaires culturelles, and went on the create the series "Civilisation du Québec." He is the co-author of *Québec, trois siècles d'architecture* and of *Québec à ciel ouvert*. He was responsible for the illustrations in the periodicals *Nos racines* and *Horizon Canada*. At Libre Expression, he is general editor of *Le Monde de Jacques Cartier* and *Ancient Canada*.

Printed in Canada